15⁰⁰
99ſ

D1060648

ANATOMY AND CONSTRUCTION
OF THE
HUMAN FIGURE

ANATOMY AND CONSTRUCTION

OF THE

HUMAN FIGURE

BY

CHARLES EARL BRADBURY

NEW YORK   TORONTO   LONDON   1949

McGRAW-HILL BOOK COMPANY, INC.

ANATOMY AND CONSTRUCTION OF THE HUMAN FIGURE

Copyright, 1949, by the McGraw-Hill Book Company, Inc. Printed in the United States of America. All rights reserved. This book, or parts thereof, may not be reproduced in any form without permission of the publishers.

I

To Vada, my wife, in gratitude
for her loyal support &
sympathetic encouragement

PREFACE

Books on figure drawing often contain fine illustrations, but the fundamental process by which they were made remains a mystery. Those who attempt to draw the human figure require an exact knowledge of the bones and muscles and of the simple principles of constructing the forms. This book is designed to meet that need.

The figure as a whole is taken up at once so that the student can make immediate application of the material in the life class. But simultaneously he constructs the figure from imagination, thus doing actual creative study from the start.

The realistic plates of bones and muscles are provided as models for study. They are shown in such views as best emphasize the true character and the function of the part. An important feature is the use of color for graphic distinction between bone, muscle, and tendon.

The numerous construction drawings show simple methods of building the forms and emphasize the fundamental character of organization.

Anatomy material has been restricted to those parts affecting the surface appearance, and scientific technical terms have been freely simplified.

Part I treats of the bones of the skeleton and their relation to the masses. Accompanying this are principles of construction in line. With the material on muscles available for reference, Part I forms a complete unit (encompassing the entire figure) for those requiring a short course.

Part II deals with the muscles and their actions. Construction is developed, and the effect of light and shade upon form is stressed.

Throughout the work, the structure of the male and female types is constantly compared.

The system presented here has been evolved by a practicing artist and art educator, originally for his own classes. Its arrangement, therefore, offers convenient adaptation to the art-school term. The book is intended also as a permanent reference work.

CHARLES EARL BRADBURY
University of Illinois

CHAMPAIGN, URBANA, ILL.

JUNE, 1949

CONTENTS

PREFACE   vii

PART I

INTRODUCTION   3

FUNDAMENTALS   5

PROPORTION   9

MOVEMENT   16

BONY STRUCTURE   20

THE HEAD I   23

THE TRUNK I   33

THE LOWER LIMB   54

THE UPPER LIMB   67

PART II

THE MUSCLES   87

THE HEAD II   90

THE FEATURES   97

THE TRUNK II   107

THE NECK   125

THE HIP   132

THE THIGH   138

THE LEG   148

THE FOOT   153

THE ARM   156

THE FOREARM   163

THE HAND   169

ACTION   177

DRAPERY   181

CONCLUSION   184

GLOSSARY   185

INDEX   193

PART I

What the basic structure of the figure actually
is & how it appears on the living form.
Construction illustrated & explained.

INTRODUCTION

THE PROBLEM. The construction of the figure cannot be learned simply *by looking at good drawings*. No amount of inspection of such material will equip one to do original work. Only by *systematic practice*, not only from life but also *from imagination*, can one acquire the ability to construct the figure.

It is necessary to know two things:

1. What the parts are actually like.
2. What are the simple principles by which they are constructed.

It is the purpose of this book to supply the essential information on these points.

Know what the parts are like; then, how they may be constructed

PROCEDURE. To learn to draw any anatomical form, study it from the chart, then attempt to draw it *from memory*. After expressing all you know, compare your drawing with the original. This will show you what you have failed to understand. Now make another memory drawing of the part and compare. This time your drawing will show more knowledge. The process should be repeated until you really have the character of the part so that you can draw it without reference to the original.

Remember that, for creative purposes, the material is of little use until you know it so thoroughly that you can represent the figure or a given part without aid of any kind.

Merely to *copy* will never give you the power to create.

The secret of progress in drawing is to apply the instructions immediately. Ultimately most students will discover the profound truths in the simple teachings, but delay is unnecessary. Endless repetition

3

of wrong methods is never a prerequisite to right study. You can begin at once to practice the methods that have been proved to be sound and that will facilitate your work. It makes no difference in what style or at what stage you are working. If you use line or pattern in any manner, you are drawing and you need all the aid you can get from sound methods of study.

The aim is to develop your creative ability

FUNDAMENTALS

NATURE OF THE HUMAN FIGURE. Though the average human figure is essentially the same as it has been for many thousands of years, in art uses it is interpreted in an infinite variety of ways. The models used by the Greek sculptors were probably not very different from those used by present-day artists. There were as greatly varied types among the peoples of that day as there are among us today. The forms of those who posed for the artists of ancient Greece were freely idealized. Form was simplified, proportions were changed, dignity was emphasized, and many details of the form were reorganized and given an arbitrary character, to suit the taste of the artist.

In all ages, even from prehistoric times, those who attempted to represent the human form must have tried to find out as much as possible about its structure. Certainly in those cases where a more or less faithful re-creation of the figure was attempted, a thorough study of its anatomy was obviously required. And for those expressions of the figure that are highly stylized, conventionalized, or abstracted, there must also be demanded enough knowledge of the human form so that it can be intelligently used as a motif for invention. Even to do a proper job of distortion, you first need to know how the figure actually is constituted.

Anyone who cannot construct the figure in its true relations certainly has not the discrimination required successfully to *alter* these relations. Creative power does not stem from ignorance or inability. To comprehend the true relations and use them require discerning vision and understanding. Attempts at mere copying of the form are

The human figure is unchanging

A thorough knowledge of the figure is a prerequisite for its use in art

5

without value, for copying is mechanical imitation, often without comprehension.

The nature of the human figure

The human figure is a complicated structure. When it is considered that there are more than 500 separate muscles in the body, some idea of its complexity may be gained. For the physician, a complete knowledge of the human body is a prerequisite. But for the artist, it is essential only to know the forms that immediately affect the external appearance.

Artist needs to know the reasons for outward appearances

Of the many muscles of the body, a large number are so thoroughly hidden as to have no appreciable effect upon the surface form. And only a small fraction of the total number actually determine this form and need to be known by the artist.

With the skeleton, the case is different. Because the bones furnish the only fixed masses on the figure, it is necessary for the artist to know most of them. But, as in the case of the muscles, of the 222 bones in the adult figure, the number that must be considered may be reduced by grouping and by taking into account the necessity of studying only those *on one side* of the skeleton.

The male figure is used as the basis of study

Throughout the book, the male figure is taken as the model for study, for the obvious reason that in the male the muscular structure attains a greater development and is more clearly defined than in the female type, in which the separation of the muscles is lost in the layer of fatty tissue—however slight—that is distributed over the surface.

This tissue gently modulates the muscular form, rounding out angles, largely eliminating the divisions between muscles, and rendering the entire form more subtle and delicate. Without it, the female form would lose its chief distinguishing characteristic and become muscular.

Anatomical shapes have the quality of design. They are of interestingly varied pattern and have an integrated relationship to one another. All form suggests plane or solid geometric figures. On the back of the trunk, triangular figures predominate; on the front, rectangles and semicircles. The neck is cylindrical, with triangles in the front. The thigh is cylindrical, with a triangle to the inside. The ovals of the head and the palm of the hand, the rectangles of the back of

The design element is conspicuous in the figure

the hips and the triangles of the feet are other examples of the geometric pattern that emphasizes character and contributes style to the form (Plate 1).

CONSTRUCTION. To conceive the form in terms of geometric shapes is a great aid to construction.

To combat the restrictions imposed by the requirement that solid form must be represented on a flat surface, *character* has to be emphasized. Otherwise, drawings will lack this vital quality. So we cannot merely copy the model. Discriminating taste needs to be cultivated, so that one may know how to make the proper selection of those features that require accentuation. This comes only from systematic study.

Construction consists in an inspection of (1) the *direction and length of the main line* of the part, (2) the *relationship of the secondary lines* to those principal ones.

Block in the *whole form* first. Then proceed to the larger divisions and lastly to the smaller parts, using plenty of fine, firm construction lines to mark all the relationships.

To keep your construction under control, never draw a form rigidly, but use light, free *suggestion* to indicate the location of parts (page 97). Give no thought to *finish*, but consider the *relation of things*. One cannot finish what has not yet been established.

The *manner* in which the drawing is done is less important than the correct *placing* of the points and lines.

As the natural tendency is to understate the form, it is necessary, on that account also, deliberately to *emphasize significant characteristics*. In the same way, some unduly obtrusive features may need to be suppressed. This use of one's artistic discrimination is a legitimate and, indeed, a vital part of one's study.

The advantage of drawing from memory or imagination is that then one can freely produce the rhythm that expresses life. In drawing from the model this is often missed, as in that case one is likely to be too intent upon following the specific form.

If you hold *clearly in mind* the character of the form you want

Emphasize CHARACTER in the forms

The nature of construction

Block in the WHOLE FORM at once

The RELATIONS between the parts are of first importance

No restrictions when one works from imagination

to construct, you can construct it. But before it can be expressed it must be *mentally conceived*.

There are various technical methods of construction at the disposal of the art student. Both straight and curved lines are equally useful. When the form is square, it is most natural to block it out in straight lines. When the forms are rounded, they may readily be swung in with ovals. Use the means best suited to the form that is to be expressed. There is no single method that is best.

In studying vertical relationships, as in the relation of the feet to the head in a standing figure, it is convincing to make tests with a plumb line. This device is simply a lead or other small weight attached to a piece of thread. Though disdained by some, it is a real help in study and deserves wider use. A reducing glass or a convex mirror is a genuine aid when a comparison is being made between the drawing and the model, as well as for revealing errors in the relations of parts. Anything that aids in the expression of form is worth while.

MATERIALS AND TECHNIQUE. For practice in drawing anatomical forms and sketching the figure in small scale, graphite drawing pencils (2H, HB, and 2B) are most convenient. A spiral sketchbook 9 by 12 inches or larger, a velvet eraser, and a sand pad are the other needs.

The harder pencil (2H) is used for light-line construction and the lighter tones, and the HB and 2B pencils, for indicating the medium and the dark tones, respectively. The lead should be cut off obliquely and worn down on the sand pad, so as to yield a broad stroke. Fine-line accents can be made with the sharp edge of the point.

The best technical methods are the natural ones

Aids to construction

Materials & their use

PROPORTION

Nature of proportion
in the figure

One of the most interesting phases of the study of anatomy is proportion. In practice, proportion is not so much something that one can measure; it is something sensed. The artist works to make his figure "look right." This seems vague but the explanation is simple. He has trained his judgment so that he instinctively recognizes just proportion, and measuring is practically unnecessary. His sensitive vision quickly detects inharmonies of space division, as a musician's ear senses discord. If spaces are correctly related, he feels that the figure "goes together." That is good proportion.

No two figures have exactly the same measurements, but a few simple proportions are needed to serve as a guide. Proportions in the figure are conveniently expressed in head lengths, and the average adult of either sex is about seven and one-half heads tall. When it is represented as seven heads or less, the type is a relatively short figure; and when eight heads are used as the height, the result is a type taller than the average. Of course, for practical purposes of expression, any of the proportions of the figure may be altered. But some standard is needed, if only to serve as a point of departure.

The male and female types will be constantly compared, in order that the characteristic differences that exist in the various parts may be clearly understood. In the larger aspect, however, the two types are strikingly distinct and we can usually distinguish unmistakably the male from the female, even at long range, where only the basic form holds. This, of course, is aside from any familiar difference of dress or of length of hair. A man and a woman bather appearing in the distance on a beach would usually be easy to differentiate. Under

*The head is
the unit of measurement*

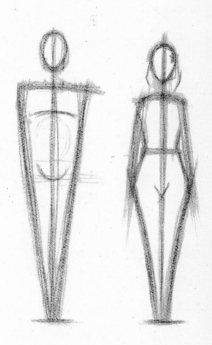

*Block forms of the
male & female types*

9

The male is heavy
ABOVE the waist
& the female is heavy
BELOW the waist

The bones furnish the
foundation of the forms

The figures of
the male & female
contrast fundamentally

such conditions, where details of form are imperceptible, it is evident that factors of a more fundamental nature are responsible for this certainty of identification. These involve big, structural differences, the most noticeable of which are the degree of development of the shoulders and chest in the man and the greater width and tilt of the hips in the woman. The male is heavy *above* the waist; the female, heavy *below*. Numerous ramifications of structure result from these two typical distinctions. They add their modifying influence upon the silhouettes and operate still further to emphasize each type. But in the main it is the evidence of physical strength associated with the male and the modifications connected with her biological function of childbearing associated with the female that actually distinguish the two types.

As always, the causes for external appearances originate in the skeleton; and the bones of the male, designed as they are to support large and powerful muscles, are in general heavier and more angular than those of the woman. Accordingly, from skull to foot, the skeleton of the female is lighter and the bones are more delicately formed than those of the man. Her rib cage is smaller in every dimension. But the female pelvis is actually wider and is also shallower than that of the male. This implies that the hip sockets are more widely separated, so that the femur, or thighbone, takes more obliquity than that of the male. Further, in the female the pelvis is more tilted.

These matters of bone character and relationship are what account most for the characteristic appearance of the types. And there is a great contrast between such extreme types as the youthful female figure and the powerfully developed athletic male. The curves of the female figure are simple and subtle. While her forms are soft and graceful, those of the male are firm and powerful. In the female form, the muscles on a given part of the anatomy are fused into one, so that the figure is characterized by long, flowing lines; while the individual masses of the strongly developed male present a series of short, blocky, convex forms. Thus the surface of the male figure is rugged and broken up, while that of the female is smooth and simple. Their opposite attributes of form make the types complementary.

THE MALE FIGURE. In the male, the middle of the figure falls at the level of the great trochanters—the widest part of the hips—so that the legs are equal in length to the head and trunk. This mid-line passes through the origin of the genitals, just below the pubis.

Several of the larger divisions of the figure equal two head lengths. They are the following:

1. From the top of the head to the line of the nipples.
2. From the nipples to the base of the hips (seen in back).
3. From the sole of the foot to the knee joint.
4. Through the widest part of the shoulders (at the fullest part of the deltoids).
5. From the clavicles to the upper iliac spine.

Other important proportions are these:

1. The width through the hips (great trochanter) equals one and one-half heads.
2. The navel is three heads down.
3. The neck is one-third of a head or more in length.
4. With the arm at the side, the hand reaches halfway down the thigh.

To fasten in thought the proportions, it is very good practice to lay out the head units with a pair of dividers, using these points as guides for drawing the figure. It is also interesting and instructive to apply the dividers to any representations of the figure for comparing their proportions.

The drawing on this page shows several stages in the construction of the type figure. Proportion and relation are secured only by working over the *whole figure* at once, not by starting at the top and

Process of construction of the male figure

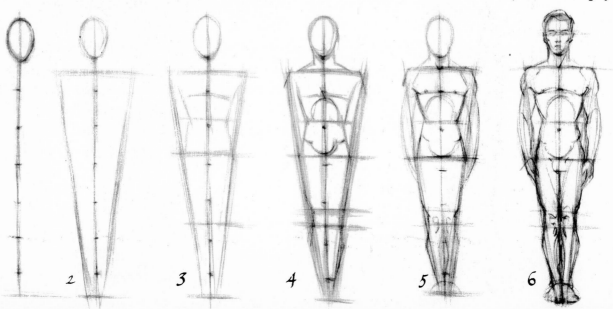

1   2   3   4   5   6

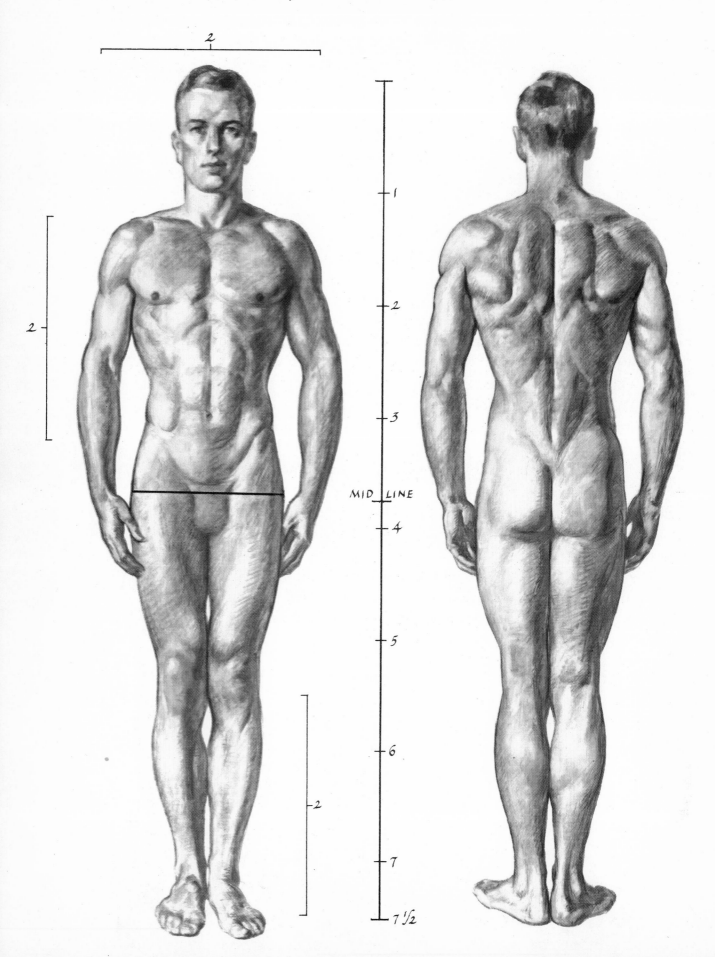

Plate I. MALE FIGURE, PROPORTIONS

2

2

2

1

2

3

MID LINE

4

5

6

2

7

7½

Plate 2. FEMALE FIGURE, PROPORTIONS

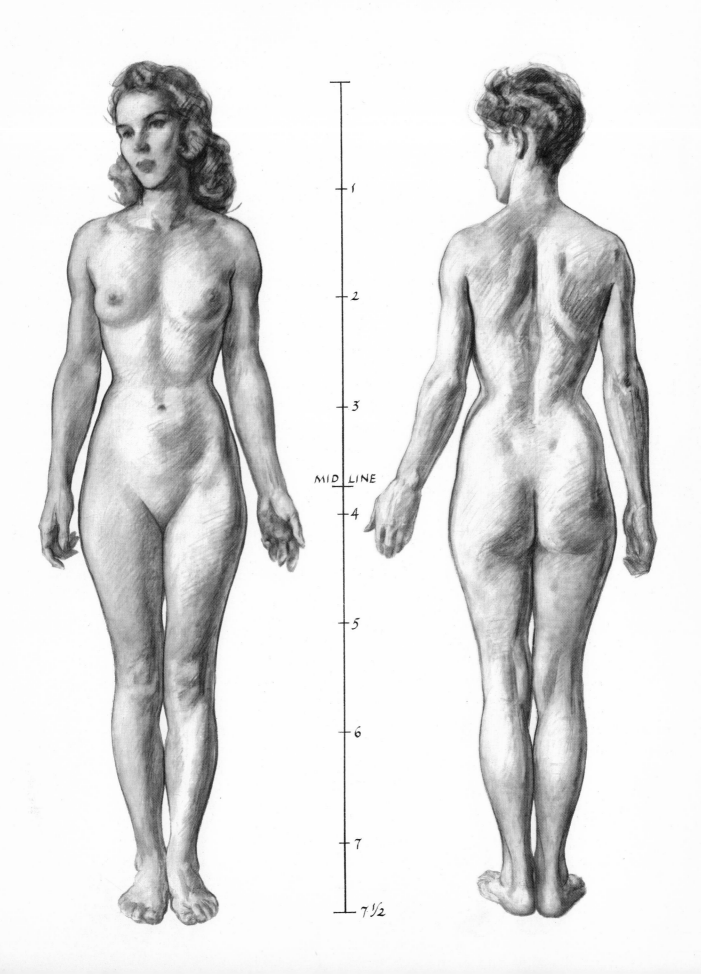

MID LINE

working down. One part is not merely added to another, but *all parts have to be coordinated*. This rule applies to all construction.

Process of construction of the male figure

1. An oval suggests the head. Through this draw an axis line and mark off the seven and one-half head units.

2. Add the triangular block form of the figure.

3. Mark off the divisions at the hips, chest, waist, and knees and suggest the wedges of the trunk and hips.

4. Block in the neck and shoulder lines, the ovals of the abdominal and hip regions, the squares of the knees, and the forms of the thighs and legs.

5. Swing in the arms. Mark the pit of the neck, nipples, navel, kneecap, and shinbones and block the foot mass.

6. Now complete the drawing by developing the forms. Suggest the features, hands, and feet.

THE FEMALE FIGURE. The female figure has many of the same general proportions as the male; but there are, of course, important differences. These are chiefly in the widths.

There are innumerable types and no two figures have exactly the same measurements, but the width through the shoulders in the female averages one and three-fourths heads.

The greatest width through the hips, which falls at a slightly lower level than in the male, is about one and five-eighths heads.

The width through the nipples and through the waist are about the same, about one head. The waistline is not much more than one-third of the way down.

In the female, the neck is longer than in the male. This is due to the smaller size of the bones above and below it (the jaw and the shoulder girdle) and also to the fact that the muscles of the shoulders, being less heavily developed, do not support the shoulders so efficiently. Again, the muscles of the neck itself are lighter and so induce the more slender appearance of the neck.

The flank of the female is longer in appearance than that of the male. The ribs, being more delicately formed and smaller, do not

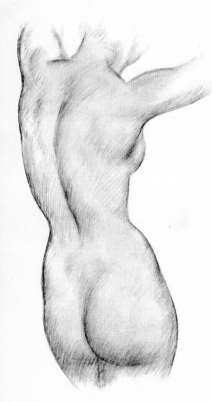

Characteristics of the female torso, back

The flank of the female is longer than that of the male

reach so far down. The pelvis, being shallower and more tipped forward, does not reach so far upward, thus leaving more space between the waist and the hips than in the male. The wide pelvis, too, projecting farther beyond the narrow thorax, creates a longer line between ribs and pelvis than in the male structure. The long hip line is augmented by the extra development of the hips in the female (pages 133 and 134).

In the female, the breasts effect a considerable modification of the chest form. The fullness of the mammary glands covers the lower and outer portions of the pectoralis (chest muscle). In both sexes, the nipples occur at the second head length. In the male, this is very close to the lower boundary of the pectoralis; but in the female, the line of the breast falls somewhat lower.

The construction of the breast forms is important. The axes of these forms are directed not only forward but also outward. In fact, their *axes are about at right angles* to the part of the chest wall from which they protrude. This means that, in the three-quarter view of the trunk, the farther breast will be seen in *profile* and the nearer one in *front view* (page 123).

The abdomen in the female is characteristically more prominent and more rounded than in the male, and the navel is more depressed (page 134).

It is interesting to compare the proportions of the infant with those of the adult. The head of the infant at birth averages about one-fourth the height of the figure. The head and trunk together equal about two-thirds of the height; and the legs, one-third.

The breasts effect a considerable modification of the chest form

Proportions of the infant

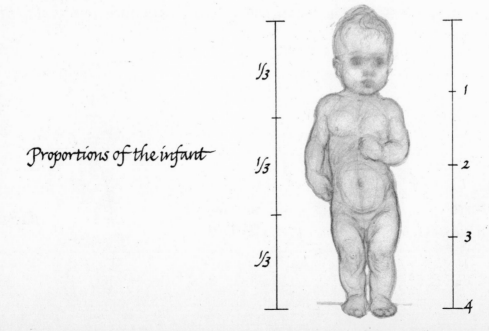

⅓ ⅓ ⅓

1 2 3 4

MOVEMENT

The essential quality of movement

In studying the proportion of the figure, for simplicity we have used only a rigid, static pose. This attitude is, of course, seldom encountered in art or in life, as life implies motion.

Movement in the human figure is called *action*. To represent this outward manifestation of life in the figure is of preeminent importance. Any rigidity in the representation robs the figure of life. There is a certain swing to the entire figure and to all its parts. To avoid a static condition, this movement needs to be sensed and applied to representations of all anatomical material, whether bones, muscles, a detail, or the complete figure.

Movement begins with the first line

The statement of movement begins with the first line, and this line comprehends the great movement of the whole figure. If there is a break in the line of movement, the rhythm is interrupted and the effect of the swing is lost. The important thing is to *make the form swing through*.

In the "normal," or straight, standing position, the masses balance one over the other, but this position is not commonly encountered in practice. More evidence of movement results when the main masses (head, thorax, and pelvis) change their relationship one to

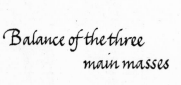

Balance of the three main masses

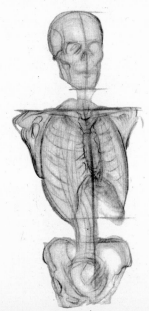

normal relation

shifted

another, and this occurs in endless variation as the figure moves naturally. Even a very relaxed sitting, leaning, or reclining posture may express strong action if the dominant, controlling line is rhythmic, or if it has variety of direction.

Action involves a change from the normal relation of the base of support to the center, or the line, of gravity of the body.

The first condition determining action is typified by a figure in which the weight is shifted so that it is distributed unequally through the feet. This involves resting the weight of the body on one leg, the opposite limb being relaxed and serving chiefly to maintain balance. While the *foot bearing the weight is directly under the head*, the position of the opposite foot may be close in, well out, forward, or back. The pose is stationary and occurs whenever the weight is shifted comfortably from one foot to the other.

Variations occur with any twisting of the body and with the disposition of the arms, which of course may assume a number of positions (page 178).

As shown in Plate 1, the figure is standing with the weight equally distributed between the feet. The axis is a vertical line that runs through the figure, dividing it symmetrically into two parts. The lines of eyes, shoulders, hips, knees, and feet are at right angles to this axis. This is the anatomical "normal" position, so named because it represents the most simple relation of the parts.

As soon as any shifting of the weight occurs, the skull, the thorax, and the pelvis are moved out of the vertical relation to one another and are tilted variously. The accompanying illustration shows such an action. The weight has been placed on the left leg, so that the left hip is forced upward. The right leg is relaxed and the knee is bent, so that the right hip falls at a lower level than the left. This gives a different sweep to the axis from hip to ankle, taking it in an oblique direction.

To compensate for the shifting of the weight as seen at the hips, the thorax must now swing to the opposite side, since balance must be maintained. Accordingly, the axis of the upper half of the figure swings back toward the line of gravity. The position of the head is

The nature of action

A shifting of the weight produces simple action

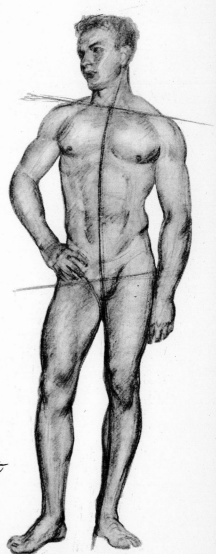

The effect of a shifting of the weight

thus maintained directly over the feet, as in the straight standing position, and balance is assured.

The resolution of the axis of the figure from the straight line into two great curves—or, more exactly, a double or reverse curve—means that the portion forming the axis of the thorax swings one way while that which forms the axis of the pelvis swings to the other side. Carrying out the balanced rhythm, the head usually tends to incline toward the high shoulder.

An important characteristic of the female figure in this action is the *concave outer border of the thigh* on the side bearing the weight. This results in a double curve in the outline from hip to ankle.

In standing figures, poses of the type described, with minor variations, are extremely frequent. When the principle of representing this action is understood, a sense of movement in the drawing is assured.

The progressive drawing on the opposite page shows several stages of the simple action figure.

The double curve expresses the essence of action

Rhythm of the figure

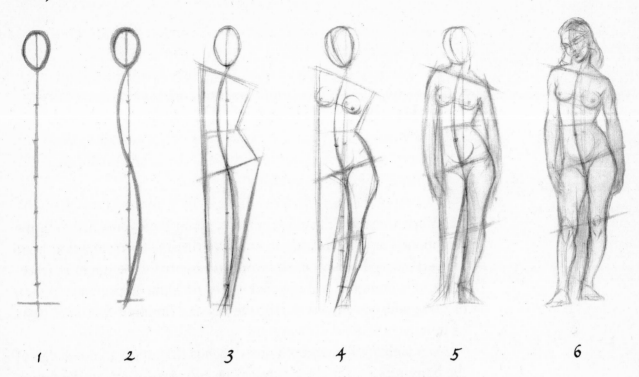

1　　　2　　　3　　　4　　　5　　　6

Stages of construction of the female figure with weight shifted

CONSTRUCTION OF FIGURE IN SIMPLE MOVEMENT

1. Draw an oval for the head and mark off the seven and one-half head divisions on the vertical axis.

2. Modify the axis by swinging in the double curve. This starts at the pit of the neck, passes through the mid-point on the axis and ends where the axis ends at the bottom.

3. Place the shoulder and hip lines and block in the figure on the axis.

4. Swing the head toward the high shoulder. Locate the breasts and indicate markings at abdomen, hips, and legs.

5. Swing in the arms, block in the feet, and develop the legs.

6. Proceed to the smaller indications: features, hair, knees, feet, and hands.

BONY STRUCTURE

*The characteristics of
bones are universal*

When we study the character of a given bone—for instance, the thighbone—it is interesting to consider that the corresponding bone in every normal person in the world is essentially the same. Furthermore, this bone has had approximately the same appearance in each of those who have lived during the last one hundred thousand years or more.

Any ability to draw the figure depends first upon a knowledge of the bony masses, for these furnish the *only fixed points* in the figure. The bones of the skeleton are bound together by ligaments, which, for the most part, have little effect upon the surface form, but which firmly unite the joints of the bony structure. The effect of the bones is apparent throughout the figure. When covered only by the skin, a bony part is said to be *subcutaneous*. In only a few regions are the muscles so massive as to conceal completely the bones beneath. But even when they lie deep, the character of the bones directly affects the outward appearance of the form. Everywhere else the bones are strongly in evidence, though usually we do not notice their presence because of our habit of seeing only the surface of the form.

Naturally the bones themselves are revealed most plainly on that subject having the least flesh, and here they appear as prominences. But even in a well-developed figure, bones are strongly marked, occurring at those points where they are covered only by the skin, as over a large portion of the head, on the backs of hands and feet, and at the important joints. In many parts, however, the powerful muscles

*Subcutaneous parts of bones
give strong surface indications*

of the strongly developed type convert the bony prominences into depressed regions.

It is surprising how much of the figure is established after we have drawn the bones that lie close to the surface. Bones furnish the basic construction lines of the figure. Particularly in head, hand, foot, front of leg, shoulder blades, rib cage, and pelvis—to a lesser degree, in the rest of the body—the bones are of first importance in the creation of the form. Joints, such as the shoulder, knee, ankle, elbow, and wrist regions, likewise owe their character primarily to the *bones* of these parts. Therefore it is that the bones come first in the study of the human form. Muscles over the bones have the effect of emphasizing their form, modifying it, as a sweater worn by the subject follows the form underneath, simplifying and augmenting it.

The skeleton consists essentially of the skull, the rib cage, and the pelvis, connected by the flexible spinal column. In the normal standing position, these are ranged one above another. To the rib cage is attached the shoulder girdle, which carries the bones of the arm, while to the pelvis are connected the bones of the thigh. With its capacity for movement, the spinal column produces innumerable changes in relation between skull, rib cage, and pelvis. And of course it is very obvious that the arms and the legs have, in themselves, great potentialities of movement.

It is necessary, then, to know the bones of the skeleton because of their effect upon the surface forms of the figure. There is a typical form underneath the superficial structure of every part of the anatomy. This form is fundamental. The cap of the shoulder is round, first because the head of the armbone is round. The knee is cubical in form because of the square shape of the bones of that region. Other examples that are quite obvious are the round form of the cranium and the oval of the rib cage.

Bones are of several sorts: long, flat, and irregular. Most of the bones of limbs are of the long type. So are ribs and collarbones. All the large bones of the skull are of the flat sort; also, the shoulder blade, the ilium, and the sacrum, as well as the kneecap and the breastbone. Many bones are of irregular shape. The vertebrae, bones

Bones furnish the basic construction lines of the figure

The three main masses are the skull, the rib cage, & the pelvis

Bones are classified as long, flat, or irregular

of wrist and ankle, small bones of the face, and the ischial bones of the pelvis are examples.

Certain terms associated with bones require defining.

1. A *process* is an ordinary prominence, or projecting part.

2. A *tuberosity* is a large prominence, usually giving attachment to muscles or ligaments.

3. A *tubercle* is similar in function to a tuberosity, but it is smaller.

4. A *condyle* is a prominence that is closely associated with the articulation of a joint.

5. A *fossa* is a shallow depression.

Terms defined

As the bones constitute the framework of the figure & provide surfaces for the attachment of muscles, their character needs to be understood .

THE HEAD I

THE SKULL. The *skull* is a marvelously adjusted unit made up of twenty-six separate bones, many of them of curious shape. But affecting the external appearance there are merely two main masses, one constituting the cranium, or skull proper, and the other, the face. For convenient reference, the main portions of each are named (Plate 3).

The skull has two main masses

Forming the forehead is the rectangular *frontal* bone. At the temples are the disklike *temporal* bones. Rounding out the top of the skull are the two *parietal* bones and at the back is the *occipital* bone.

For our purpose, these six bones constitute the cranium. They form one mass, being immovably fitted together by serrated joinings, which have no effect upon the form, but allow expansion during the growth of the skull.

There are six essential bones in the skull

In these skull bones there are certain surface variations that are important to the artist. Their thin coverings of muscle tend only to emphasize them. On the upper part of the forehead are two prominences, called *frontal eminences*. These are quite characteristic features of the female head, but are less important in the male.

Just above the inner corners of the eye sockets are the prominent *superciliary eminences*, which are definitely male characteristics.

At the side, the *temporal ridge* accentuates the division between the top and side planes of the skull.

The prominences on the skull

Another important surface form is the prominent *mastoid process*. This can readily be felt just behind the ear. It is less noticeable in the child.

The chief bones of the face are the cheekbones (*malar* bones), the

23

Plate 3. SKULL

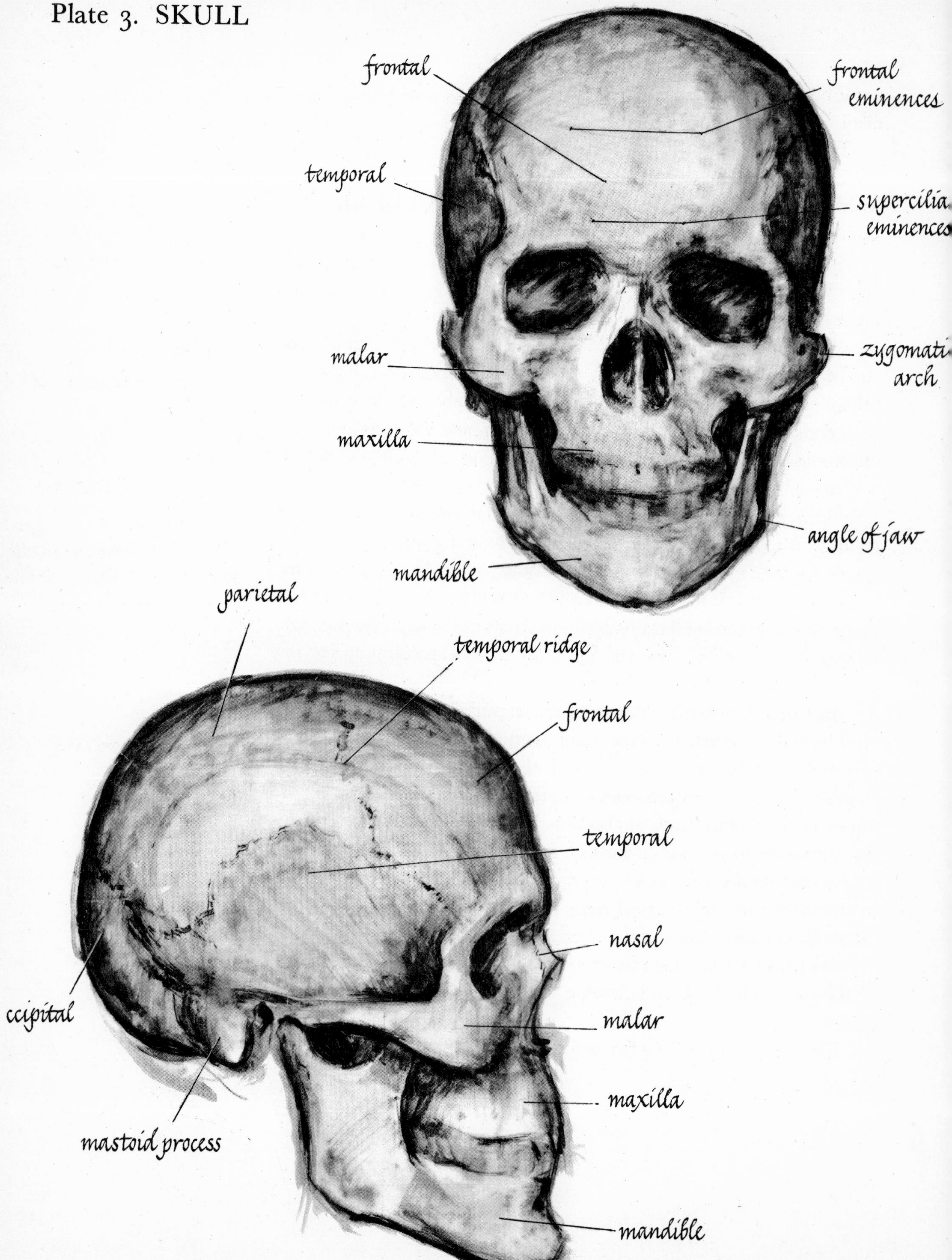

frontal

frontal eminences

temporal

supercilia eminences

malar

zygomatic arch

maxilla

angle of jaw

mandible

parietal

temporal ridge

frontal

temporal

nasal

malar

maxilla

ccipital

mastoid process

mandible

nasal bones, and the *maxilla*. These, like the bones of the skull, are firmly welded together by fixed joints, called *sutures*.

The *mandible* forms the jaw and the chin. It articulates with the skull just in front of the ear opening by a joint that combines hinge with grinding action. This is the only movable joint on the entire skull (Plate 23).

Bridging the space from the cheekbone to the temporal is the *zygomatic arch*. It runs straight back from the level of the bottom of the eye socket. Its lower boundary runs downward and forward, paralleling the jaw.

The large squared hollows forming the orbits for the eyes are the primary depressions on the skull, the nasal opening not being a factor in the head because it is covered by the projecting cartilage that forms the lower half of the nose.

Secondary depressions are those under the cheekbone and the zygomatic arch and that above the arch over the temple—the *temporal fossa*.

CONSTRUCTION OF THE SKULL.

As is indicated in the drawing, the skull is essentially a spherical form, with a wedge-shaped lower portion. The essence of its form is expressed by four prominences—the forehead, two cheekbones, and the chin—with the large depressed areas of the eye sockets.

The maxilla forms, with the mandible, one semicylindrical plane, of which the teeth are a part.

The face is somewhat longer than the cranium, the midline from top of skull to chin being at the lower part of the eye sockets, *i.e.*, the line of the lower lid, on the model.

A characteristic of man is the practically vertical axis of the skull. In animals of similar structure, as the dog, the horse, or even the ape, the skull is formed so that its axis approaches the horizontal. Another human characteristic is the extraordinary development of the cranium.

The art student cannot become too familiar with the skull. Know its simple block form, so that you can draw it in any position. This is the first step in drawing the head.

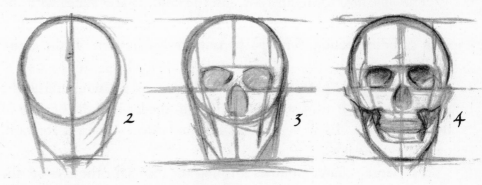

Method of constructing the skull

Stages in the construction of the skull

1. A circle suggests the cranium.

2. Draw the axis, adding one-third of a diameter for the wedge of the lower skull, and block this in.

3. Draw the midline. Put in the eye sockets so that their lower boundary falls on the midline. Add the nasal opening and the division between the maxilla and the mandible.

4. Block out the cheekbones along the circle. Suggest the planes of the teeth and the front and side planes of the cranium. Indicate the depressions by shadows.

The side view follows a similar sequence.

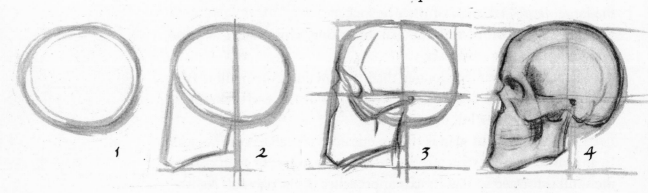

PROPORTIONS OF THE FACE. The natural divisions of the face are three:

1. From the hairline to the brows.

2. From the brows to the base of the nose.

The three divisions of the face

3. From the base of the nose to the base of the chin.

These average about equal, but any head would show variations in its proportions that would give it individuality. However, these three similar zones of the face are conveniently comparable in construction.

There are innumerable small details of form in the features, which can best be observed from life. But the main prominences and depressions, the changes of plane, and other general characteristics will be noted here.

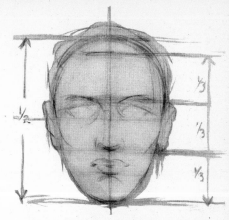

Proportions of the head, front

PLANES. The forehead is definitely squared, the front plane extending to the line of the eye sockets, where it turns abruptly into the plane of the temple. The front plane is subdivided by transitional planes, whose boundaries run from the frontal eminences to the superciliary eminences. There are irregularities in the modeling of the central portion, caused by these latter prominences and the flat area between them. The strongest light on the head is usually found on the forehead.

In the middle zone of the head are the eye sockets, the cheekbones, the nose, and the ears.

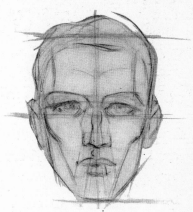

The planes of the head

PROMINENCES AND DEPRESSIONS. The cheekbones are fully as important to the face as is any other feature, for they are determinants of contour. They extend upward and outward, outside the socket. With the prominences of forehead and chin, the cheekbones are the "high spots" of the face. Covered only by the skin, they reflect the light and constitute two of the main high lights of the head. Nothing contributes more to the character of form in the head than do the cheekbones.

From the cheekbones to the ear runs the ridge of the zygomatic arch, marking the change of plane between the temple and the jaw.

The jaw projects from underneath the cheekbones and has an angular character, which contrasts with the round forms above. Forms of the jaw carry out the rhythm of the head. The head is a combination of rounded and squared forms.

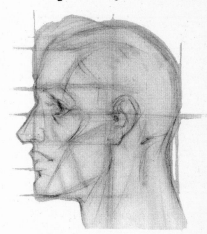

The planes from the side

Prominences & depressions

Advancing & retreating planes give alternate light & shade

Breaking the advancing front plane are a series of retreating planes: eye sockets, end of nose, upper red lip, under surface of lower lip, and end of chin.

Each individual feature has its own system of planes.

The fundamental nature of the skull in the appearance of the head is illustrated in a simple way by the drawings above. It will be noted that the essentials of form in the face are not dependent upon a finished rendering of the head, but that they are largely suggested in the sketch of the skull alone.

CONSTRUCTION OF THE HEAD. Various concepts of the head form the basis of its construction. For the front view, a free oval suggests its general shape, from which the form is developed. As with the human figure, a combination of curved and straight lines offers the most possibilities.

As a solid form, the head appears sometimes more ovoid, sometimes more cubical, according to type. For an understanding of the

The oval suggests the head

Construction of the head

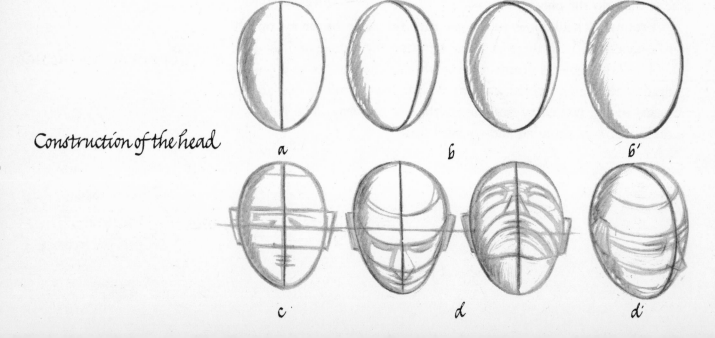

a   b   b'

c   d   d'

principles involved in representing the head in certain positions, the ovoid is the simplest basic form. The first line swinging in the form is free—merely establishing the general feeling of the form in space.

From directly in front, a line drawn over the curved surface of the ovoid at its middle appears straight (*a*).

But if the ovoid solid is turned, the line is seen curving over the surface (*b*) until, if it is turned farther, the line approaches the outline of the ovoid (*b'*) and finally would be absorbed by it.

Similarly, lines drawn horizontally over the curved surface of the ovoid are straight lines when the ovoid is directly in front of the observer and in an upright position (*c*).

But when the ovoid is tipped forward or backward, such lines follow the curved surface of the solid (*d*).

The front view of the head is based upon (*a*) and (*c*); the three-quarter view, upon (*d'*); and the side view, upon (*b'*). The head tilted forward or backward is based upon (*d*).

ACTION. When the head tips forward or backward, it moves on an axis that would run through the middle of the head, or about through the ear openings.

As the ears are on such an axis, their positive location is little altered by the tipping of the head. But the relation of the features to the line of the ears changes enormously with these movements and, when the head is tipped forward, the entire face may fall below the line of the ears. When the head is tipped backward, the face falls well above this line (see also pages 125, 126, 129, and 179).

Lines drawn over the ovoid follow the curve of its form

The ear axis is the key to tipping movements of the head

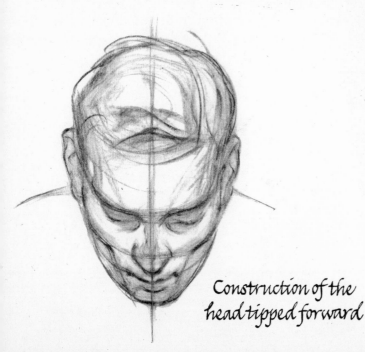

Construction of the head tipped forward

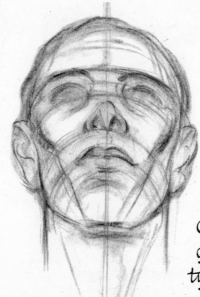

Construction of the head tipped backward

In block form,
the head is like the cube

Distinguish between
opposing planes

In drawing, there is always the necessity of a careful separation of planes. The cube immediately expresses planes. A square accurately gives the block form of the head from the side.

Any given surface of the face must be defined as belonging either to front, side, upper, or under plane system; for, like the cube, the head has six sides. Though these are unequal and modified, still the drawing or modeling of the head depends primarily upon distinguishing radically between planes.

Roughly, the front plane, slanting slightly forward, comprises forehead, cheeks, mouth, and chin. The mass of the nose grows from this plane. The side of the head and the face is at right angles to the front plane, the general boundary passing down the temple, around the cheekbone, and then to just outside the corner of the mouth.

The large, main planes can be subdivided in a variety of ways, and this gives the individual quality to each head. For the three-quarter view of the head, the cube turned at an angle suggests the planes. The line bounding the front and side planes, from the temple to the chin, is found by reference to the outline on the outer side of the face, for this is a similar boundary.

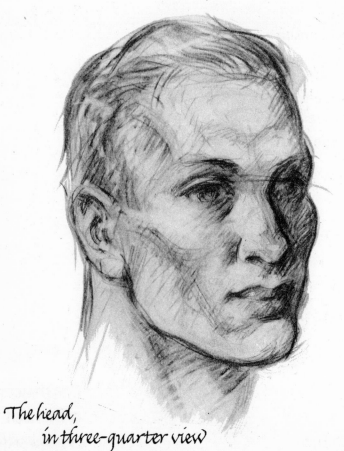

Boundary lines of
corresponding planes balance

The head,
in three-quarter view

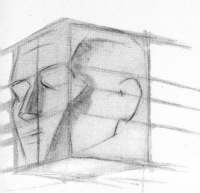 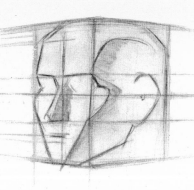 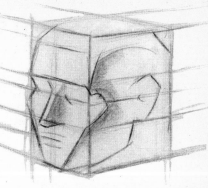

PERSPECTIVE. Particularly when perspective is a strong factor, as in the three-quarter view of the head placed above or below the eye level, the cube is most useful for the comprehension of the conditions; for, with its opposing planes at right angles to each other, the head suggests the cube.

In problems such as these, careful thought as to the *relative direction of the lines* is essential.

There is always perspective, or foreshortening, and when the head is partly turned, two sets of planes are in perspective. On these planes, the retreating lines of features are in perspective and so will converge with all such lines. If the position of the head is below the level of the eye, the lines run upward to this level; if above, they run downward.

RELATION OF NECK TO HEAD. From the front, the lines of the neck go straight down from the sides of the jaw. The cylindrical neck is modified by three triangular planes, which are buttressed by two others. In profile, the neck goes back on a slant. It is attached well back on the skull. Bounded by the jaw and shoulder lines, the block form of the neck in side view is rectangular.

The perspective of the cube applies to the head

Observe the RELATIVE DIRECTION *of the lines*

The lines of the neck go straight down from the jaws

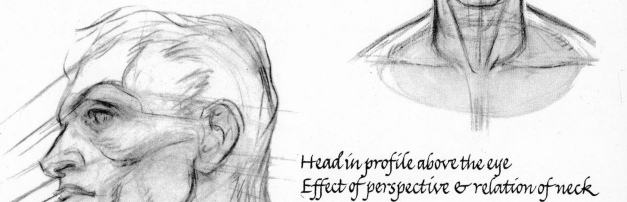

Head in profile above the eye Effect of perspective & relation of neck

The neck is attached WELL BACK *on the skull*

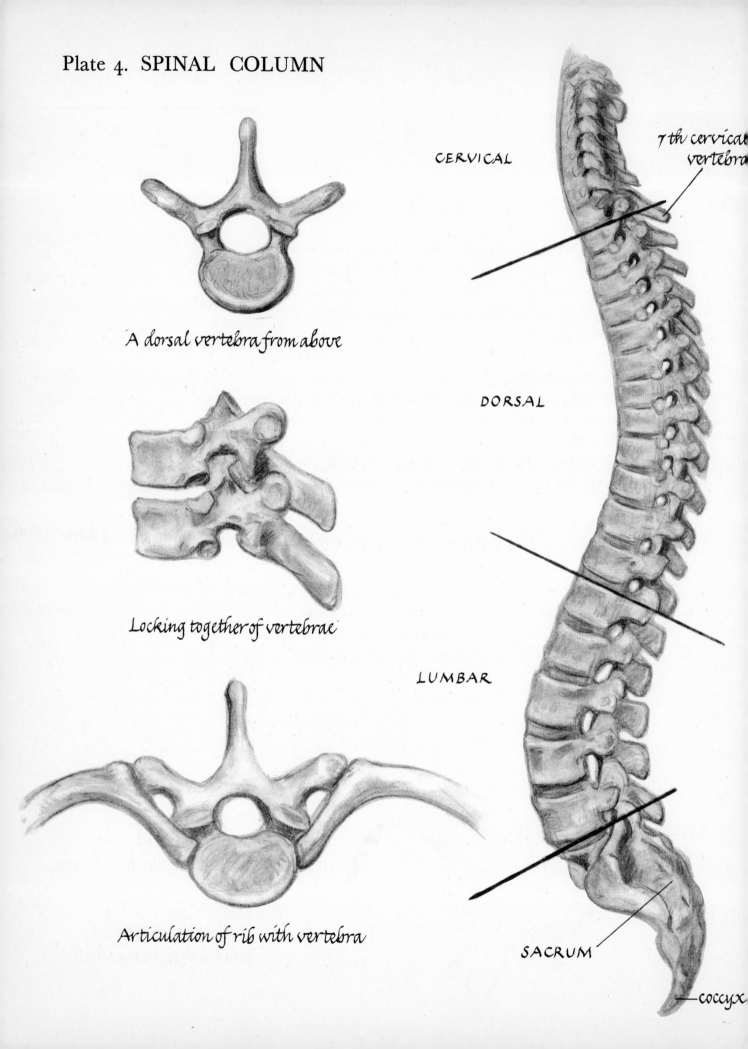

Plate 4. SPINAL COLUMN

A dorsal vertebra from above

Locking together of vertebrae

Articulation of rib with vertebra

CERVICAL

7th cervical vertebra

DORSAL

LUMBAR

SACRUM

coccyx

THE TRUNK I

In order to understand the causes of important surface appearances, it is necessary to know the bone structure; for many indications of form are so delicately presented on the model that, unless he knows what to look for, the student may fail to recognize significant features and consequently will bungle his interpretation. To the artist who knows, crudities in drawing are quickly detected.

THE SPINAL COLUMN. The spinal column forms the bony axis of the trunk and connects the three principal masses of the skeleton: skull, rib cage, and pelvis.

The column is composed of 24 vertebrae. These vertebrae are circular, disklike bones, set one above another, with a pad of elastic cartilage between.

Three spines radiate from each vertebra. Two project outward and one backward. The lateral spines articulate with the ribs. The spines also provide surfaces for the attachment of the powerful muscles of the back, extending from hips to skull—muscles that straighten the trunk, holding it erect.

The skull is carried by the topmost vertebra, which is ring-shaped and provided with two flat disks, on which the skull rests and may rock backward and forward, as in nodding movements. This vertebra is called the *atlas*.

The vertebrae of the neck (*cervical vertebrae*) are seven in number. Their spines slant sharply downward. On the model they are usually obscured by the muscles of the region. The last, or *seventh*, cervical vertebra, however, is important on the surface. It projects sharply,

The bone structure discloses WHAT TO LOOK FOR *on the figure*

The spinal column forms the axis of the trunk

In the neck are seven vertebrae

The seventh cervical vertebra is a landmark

appearing as a prominence and furnishing one of the main landmarks along the spine. Its position is of importance to the artist, because it marks the lower boundary of the neck in back, the division between neck and shoulder; also because of its relation to the pit of the neck.

The *middle,* or *dorsal,* section of the column is composed of 12 vertebrae, which give attachment to the 12 ribs on each side. The manner of their attachment to the lateral spines of these 12 vertebrae is shown in Plate 4. These dorsal vertebrae follow a convex line, determining the oval of the rib cage. They form a groove, except when the trunk is bent forward, and the ends of the lower spines are projected.

There are five large vertebrae forming the *lumbar* region. As they make the transition between the rib cage and the pelvis, these must be strong. No other bony mass occurs here. The direction of the line bordering the lumbar vertebrae is concave backward, thus balancing the convex curve of the dorsal region above.

The column is terminated by the *sacrum,* through which articulation with the pelvis is effected. The sacrum is a heavy, beaklike form. It was used in ancient sacrifices, from which fact is derived its name. The vertebrae of which the sacrum is composed are fused into one solid mass, but the lowest of these vertebrae forms the apex of an inverted triangle, the sacroiliac triangle, an important structural form at the base of the spine. The tip of the sacrum is made up of several small, spineless vertebrae, forming the *coccyx,* which terminates the spine.

It will be observed how accurately the column expresses the line of the trunk in the profile. The column is a unit and its four curves are characteristic of man. They are evolved through the effort to carry the body erect. In infancy only one curve exists but, as the child gradually progresses from the horizontal to the erect position, the column develops changes in direction. These are incident to the

The twelve vertebrae of the back connect with the ribs

Five vertebrae make the transition between the rib cage & the pelvis

The sacrum connects with the pelvis

Relation of spinal column to trunk

The column determines the four curves on the back line

Effect of spinal column in the infant

Effect of spinal column in the aged

*In the aged, the column may revert
to the one curve of infancy*

necessity of keeping the body's center of gravity over the base of support, thus maintaining balance.

As age advances, the column tends gradually to revert to the one curve of infancy.

The flexible column provides movement in every direction: forward, backward, sidewise, and rotary. The greatest movement is in the cervical and lumbar regions. Backward bending is limited by the meeting of the projecting vertebrae (pages 177, 178, and 179).

*The column has
great range of movement*

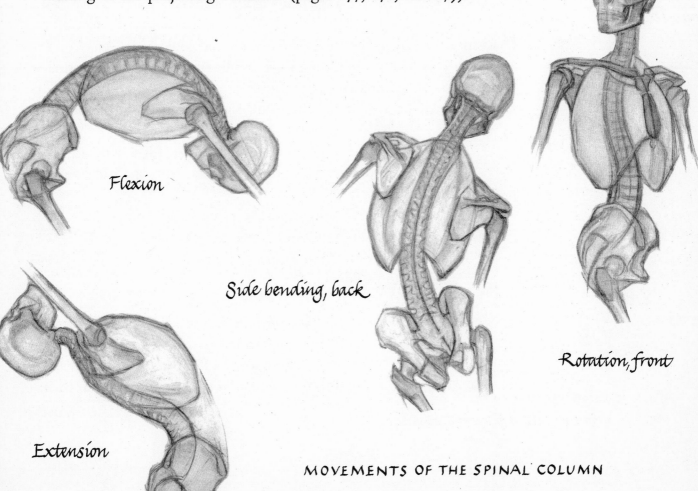

Flexion

Side bending, back

Rotation, front

Extension

MOVEMENTS OF THE SPINAL COLUMN

Construction of
the figure in profile

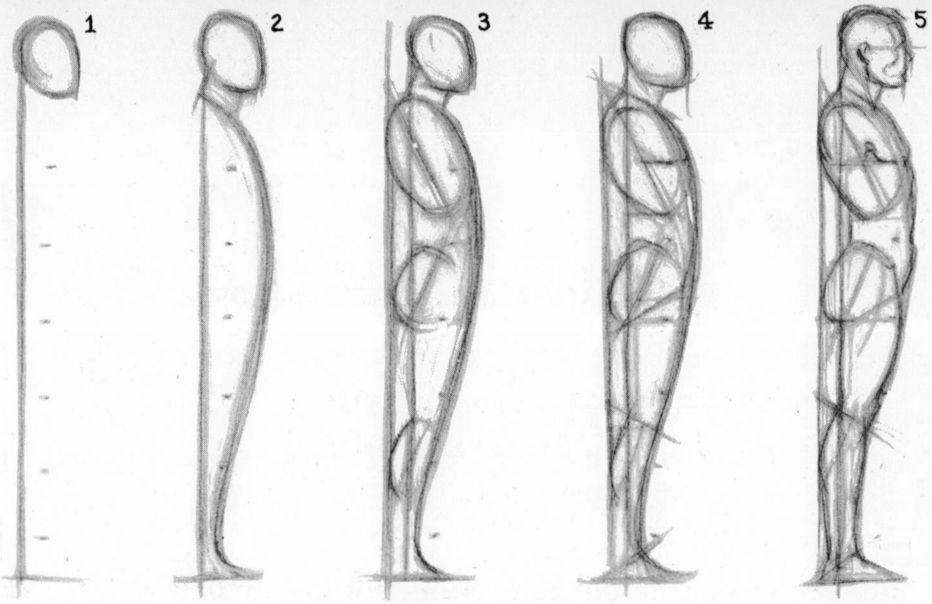

In the side view of the figure, the symmetry of the front and the back gives way to a more active expression of form.

The simple double curve down the front of the figure is the basic line. This is opposed by the variety of direction in the lines of the back.

Process of construction of the male figure in profile

1. Place the oval of the head. Mark its relation to the feet by a vertical line from the back of the skull and indicate the head divisions. This line passes through the middle of the ankle and approximates the back boundary of the thigh.

The sweep
down the front
is balanced by
the variety of
the back boundary

2. Attach the neck at a backward slant and sweep in the double curve.

3. Place the axes for the ovals of the thorax, hips, and calf and swing them in. Prominences of the shoulders, hips, and calf line up in vertical relation.

4. Mark the lateral relations at chest, hip, knee, and ankle.

5. Develop the head, lines of trunk, leg, and foot.

The typical sweep of the forms in the profile view is illustrated on pages 107, 139, and 149.

THE RIB CAGE. The *rib cage* is the second of the three principal masses of the body. It is of simple ovoid form, with the small end at the neck. The cage is composed of the 24 ribs, which are articulated with the 12 dorsal vertebrae of the spinal column in back

The foundation
of the trunk is the oval rib cage

Plate 5. RIB CAGE, FROM FRONT & SIDE

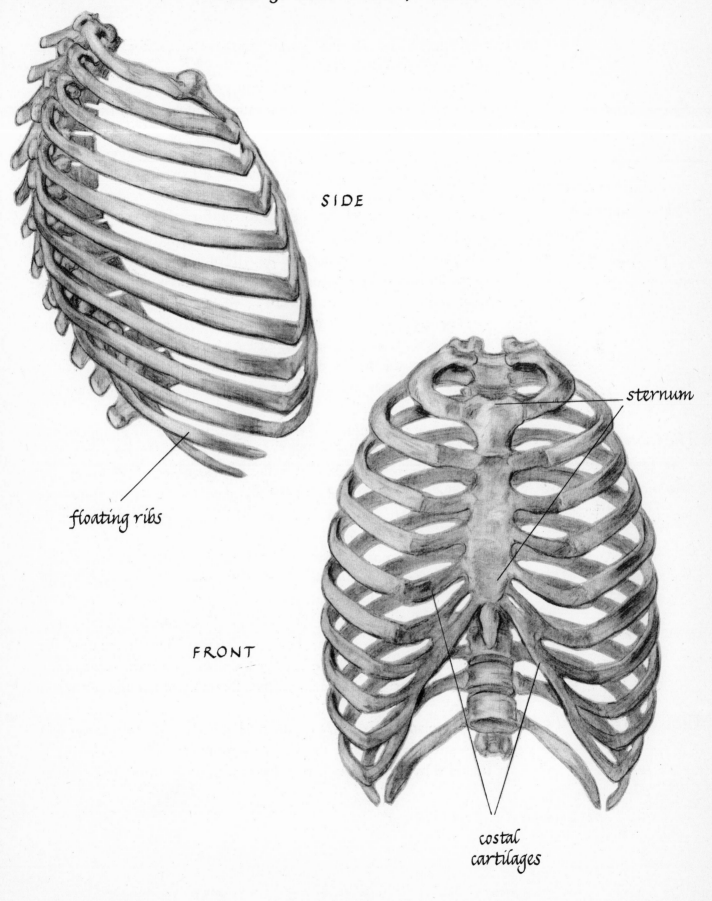

SIDE

FRONT

floating ribs

sternum

costal
cartilages

and attached by cartilage to the breastbone in front (except the eleventh and twelfth ribs).

Each rib is firmly connected with its corresponding dorsal vertebra by articular surfaces on both the lateral spine and the body of the vertebra, as shown in Plate 5.

From the spinal column, the rib starts backward, downward, and outward to its angle, where it turns toward the front of the body. The angles, therefore, form the boundaries of the middle plane of the back. The rib reaches nearly to the breastbone, to which it is attached by a length of cartilage. The cartilages for the first seven ribs give direct attachment; the next three have their cartilages connected to those of the rib next above, and the last two have no connection to the breastbone and are called *floating ribs*.

The upper ribs, therefore, form a less flexible mass than do the lower ones. However, the whole cage expands and contracts easily by reason of the flexible cartilage insertion at the front.

Intercostal muscles fill the spaces between the ribs, making the cage a complete shell.

The upper portion of the cage is greatly modified in appearance by the shoulder girdle, which fits over it, but the lower part determines the form of the lower trunk. The cartilages of the lower ribs give the characteristic line to the abdominal arch, which completes an oval with the curved boundary of the abdomen below. This is best seen when the chest is expanded.

In the erect posture from the side, the axis of the cage runs downward and forward. The axis in back corresponds to the spinal column and, in front, to the breastbone.

The individual ribs are flat. The set of the ribs follows the contour of the oval space that the cage encloses. Thus the longest, the seventh, rib has its flat side in a vertical plane, while the plane of the first rib is nearly horizontal and the eleventh and twelfth are tipped inward.

The planes of the rib cage are well defined, and in the lower half they strongly influence the surface appearance. The back plane is bounded by a line on each side that swings down through the angles

Elastic cartilage, connecting ribs to breastbone, provides flexibility

The form of the cage is modified by the shoulder girdle

The planes of the ribs

Plate 6. RIB CAGE, FROM BACK, & STERNUM

STERNUM

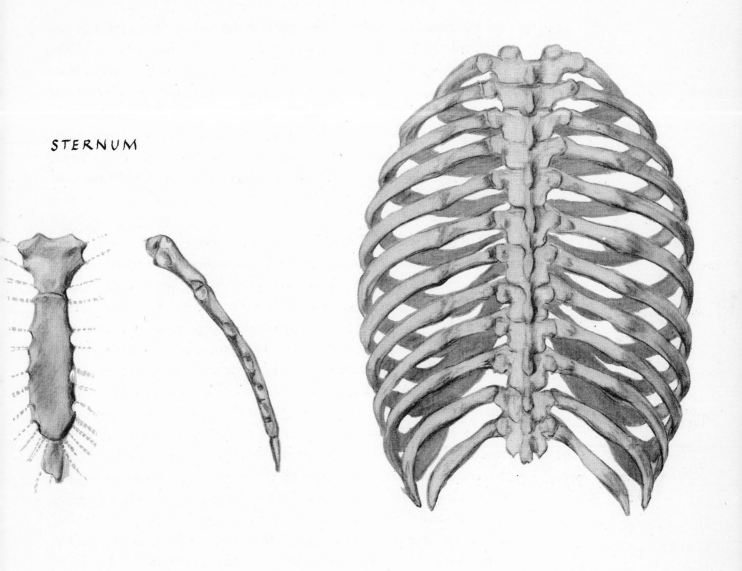

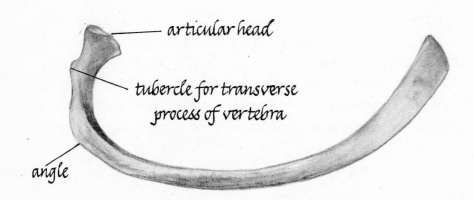

articular head

tubercle for transverse
process of vertebra

angle

6th RIB FROM ABOVE

of the ribs. In front, the lines follow the points of junction of the ribs with their cartilages (pages 108 and 122). The shoulder girdle, however, greatly broadens the middle plane both in front and in back.

Since it is typically ovoid in shape, the general form of the rib cage may be conveniently expressed by long, sweeping curved lines. As the ribs start higher at the back, the curve of the ribs is downward to the front. The back view shows them curving upward, and from the side they run obliquely downward.

THE BREASTBONE. The breastbone, or *sternum*, could serve as the model for the original four-in-hand tie. It has a knot-shaped segment which, in profile, makes a slight angle with the long portion. The sternum is usually likened to a dagger, with handle, blade, and point. Its upper boundary is hollowed and with the ends of the collarbones forms the pit of the neck. This is an important point on the figure, since it is where the backward-sloping neck ends and the forward-sloping chest begins. The upper segment of the sternum is prominent, blending with the general convexity of the upper chest; but the blade portion appears as a depressed groove between the chest muscles. At the lower end of the sternum, there is a short appendage whose prominence marks the pit of the stomach.

As indicated, the sternum gives attachment to the ribs: to seven of them on either side directly and to three indirectly. Its length, without the appendage, is about six inches, which is comparable to the length of the shoulder blade and of the collarbone.

The sternum is entirely subcutaneous. The evidence of the sternum on the surface is of special interest, because it forms the front axis of the figure in this region.

SHOULDER GIRDLE. As we have seen, the rib cage affords no means of attachment for the armbone. Therefore, other mechanism is required. This is provided by the *shoulder girdle* and is made up of the *scapulae*, or shoulder blades, and the *clavicles*, or collarbones. The girdle encircles the top of the rib cage and is de-

Character in the cage is expressed by the DIRECTION of the ribs

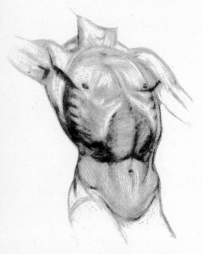

Relation of the rib cage to the trunk, front

The upper boundary of the sternum marks the pit of the neck

Relation of the rib cage to the trunk, side

Plate 7. SHOULDER GIRDLE

FROM ABOVE

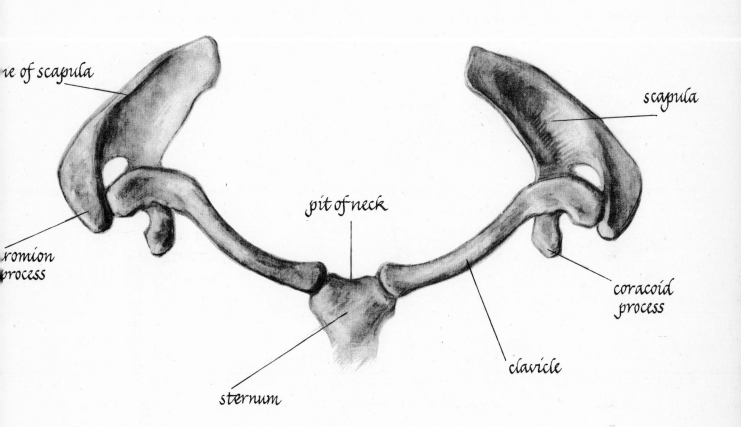

e of scapula

scapula

pit of neck

romion
process

coracoid
process

clavicle

sternum

clavicles

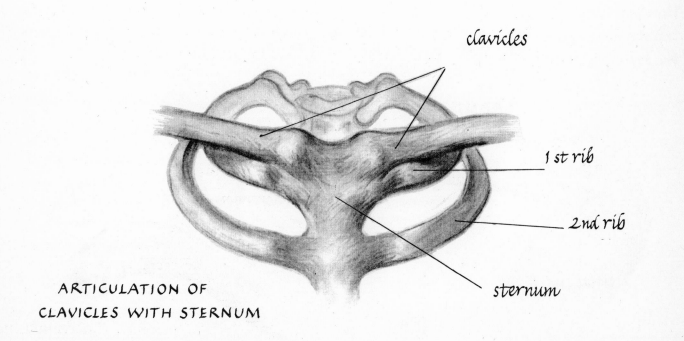

1st rib

2nd rib

sternum

ARTICULATION OF
CLAVICLES WITH STERNUM

Plate 8. SCAPULA & CLAVICLE

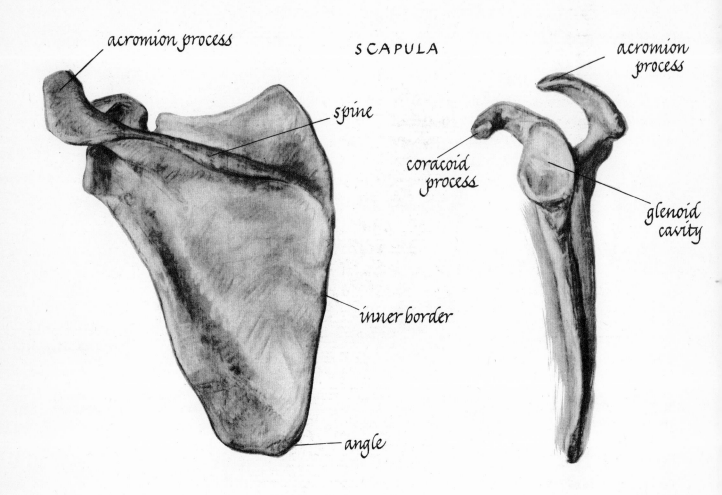

acromion process

SCAPULA

acromion process

spine

coracoid process

glenoid cavity

inner border

angle

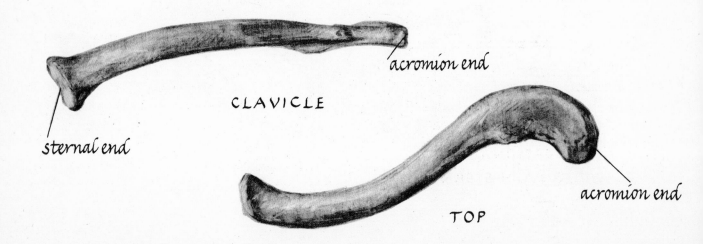

FRONT

acromion end

CLAVICLE

sternal end

acromion end

TOP

The shoulder girdle carries
the arm bones & gives
attachment to muscles

signed to carry the bones of the arm and to provide surfaces for lodgment of muscles that move the arm. Around the shoulder there is a complete circle of radiating muscles. The effect of this structure, fitting over the rib cage, is to *square the form* of the upper trunk.

THE SCAPULA. The *scapula* is triangular in form and is slightly hollowed within, to fit over the curve of the rib cage, on which it glides. It has the spring necessary to allow the extremely free movement required in the upper limb.

Important for its effect upon the surface is the *spine of scapula*, a projecting ridge running obliquely from the upper part of the inner border of the scapula and hooking around to form the cap of the shoulder. Here it is known as the *acromion process* and it bevels toward the back. With the *coracoid process*, a smaller projection at the front, the acromion forms the shallow cavity for the armbone, called the *glenoid cavity*. A large part of the scapula is concealed by muscle, but its *inner border* and its *spine* strongly affect the appearance of the back.

*Surface indications
of the scapula*

*The spine
& inner edge of the
scapula are subcutaneous*

THE CLAVICLE. The *clavicle,* with its mate, extending across the top of the chest in a straight line to the shoulders, actually takes the shape of an S curve when seen from above. Thus it is made to conform to the curve of the rib cage. As it swings on past the cage, the clavicle broadens and turns forward, to articulate with the acromion process of the scapula, completing the girdle of the shoulder.

The girdle has on each side only one point of articulation with the rib cage. This joint is at the front of the girdle, where the clavicle joins the sternum. No other bony connection between the shoulder girdle and the rib cage exists. Only by muscle are other connections made between the girdle and the rib cage. Such loose construction makes possible a remarkable degree of movement.

The clavicles and the first two ribs are represented as they appear when bound to the sternum by ligaments.

The clavicles, which are completely subcutaneous, provide an im-

*Loose joining of
girdle & cage
allows great
freedom of movement*

The clavicles mark the line of the shoulders

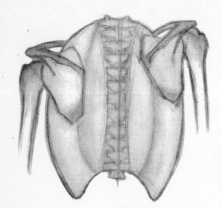

Raised

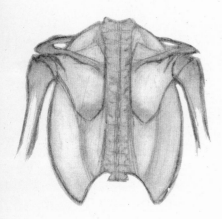

Drawn backward

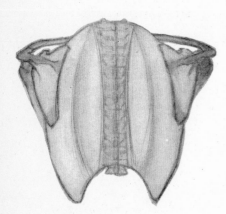

Drawn forward

portant structural line for marking the relation of the shoulders.

In Plate 9 the shoulder girdle, carrying the armbones, has been applied to the rib cage, and the region is shown in complete form. Here the articulation of the armbone, or *humerus*, in the glenoid cavity, as well as other important relationships, may be studied.

MOVEMENTS OF THE SHOULDER GIRDLE.

The back is subjected to constant changes in appearance with every movement of the arm, since the arm is carried by the shoulder girdle. The same is true in a degree of the front of the trunk, where the clavicle is seen as it moves with the arm.

There can be no appreciable movement of the arm without simultaneous movement of the shoulder girdle.

The head of the armbone works in the glenoid cavity formed by the two processes of the scapula, the acromion and the coracoid. As the armbone moves upward, its head exerts pressure beneath the acromion, pushing it up and rotating the whole scapula. Thus the scapula moves with the arm.

Not only is the arm capable of free movement in the shallow cavity at the shoulder, but added to this is the movement contributed by the rotating scapula.

At the shoulder, the varieties of movement are many. The shoulders may be pushed up or depressed. They may be drawn forward or backward. In all these movements, as well as in that of raising the arm, the scapula glides over the rib cage or may even be partly drawn away from it. Muscles by which it is attached to the rib cage limit the various movements.

It will be understood that, with each movement, certain muscles are stretched in different degrees and directions, while others are

Rotated, front

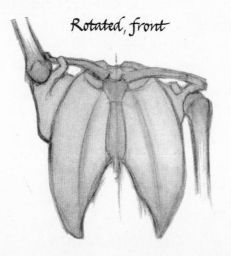

Rotated, back

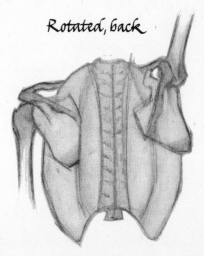

Plate 9. SKELETON OF THE UPPER TRUNK

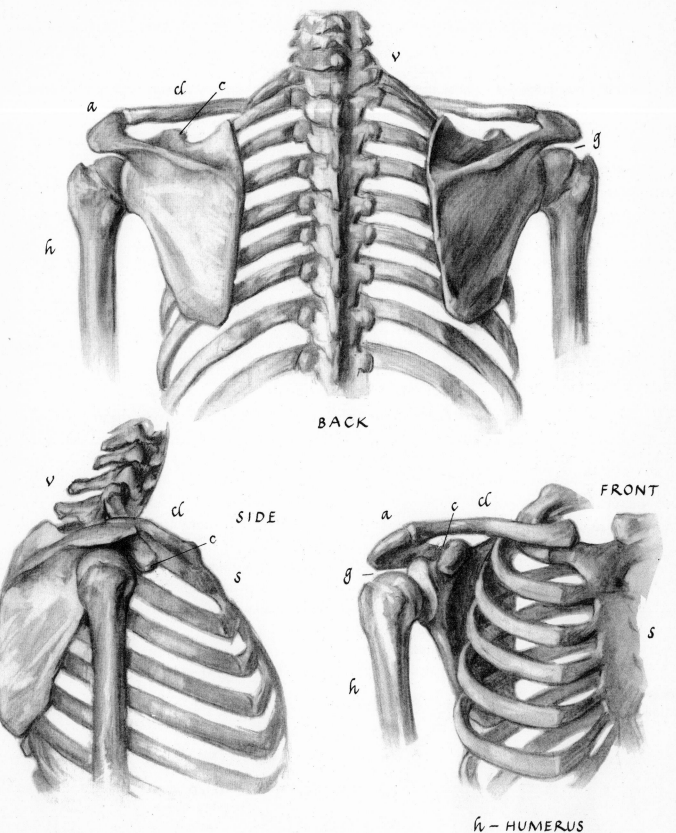

BACK

SIDE

FRONT

a — ACROMION PROCESS   cl — CLAVICLE   h — HUMERUS

c — CORACOID PROCESS   g — GLENOID CAVITY   s — STERNUM

                                                       v — 7th CERVICAL VERTEBRA

contracted variously. Besides, there are innumerable combinations of movements affecting the appearance of the back. For example, when the shoulders are drawn forward, the scapulae are widely separated and the rib cage, with its thin covering of stretched muscles, is exposed between them. When the shoulders are drawn back, the inner edges of the two blades might meet, were it not for the thickness of the intervening muscles which are now contracted.

From the front, too, the effect of shoulder and arm movement is considerable. If the arm is raised beyond the horizontal, the scapula is rotated outward beyond the side of the rib cage, thus modifying the shape of this mass of the trunk. The clavicle, also, is raised at the outer end and so runs upward from the pit of the neck (Plate 32). Again, when the shoulders are drawn back, the clavicles more nearly conform to the curve of the chest wall, while in the forward position their outer ends are drawn forward and cause a hollowing of the chest.

THE HIP GIRDLE. Just as the shoulder girdle provides attachment for the armbones, so the hip girdle carries the thighbones. But unlike the shoulder girdle, which is loosely joined so that free movement is permitted, the girdle of the hips is a complete ring, solidly welded to the spinal column; for here strength and stability are required to provide a firm seating for the thighbones, through which the whole weight of the body is transmitted.

The hip girdle, or *pelvis,* is the last of the three main masses of the skeleton. It is an irregular mass, much of which is imbedded in the heavy muscles of the hips. It is made up of three parts in one: *ilium, ischium,* and *pubis.* In infancy these are three separate bones, but in the adult they are fused into one.

From the top, the basketlike shape formed by the large iliac bones, joined at the back by the wedging in of the sacrum and in front by

Relations in front are altered by movements of the shoulder girdle

The hip girdle carries the thighbones

Movements of the shoulder girdle cause changes in the forms on the back

inner border of scapula

spine of scapula

acromion process

EFFECT OF THE SHOULDER GIRDLE ON THE TRUNK

lower angle of scapula

Plate 10. PELVIS OR HIP GIRDLE

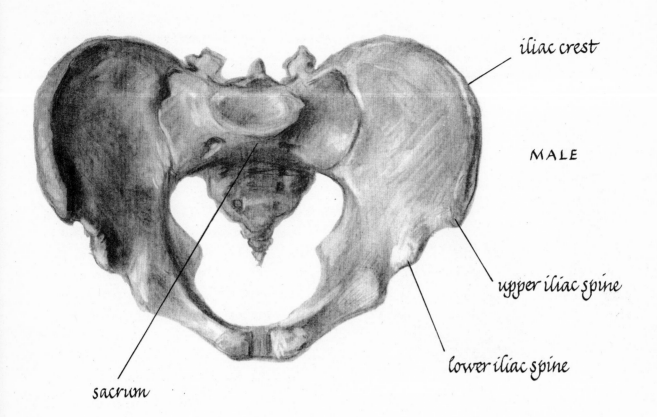

iliac crest

MALE

upper iliac spine

lower iliac spine

sacrum

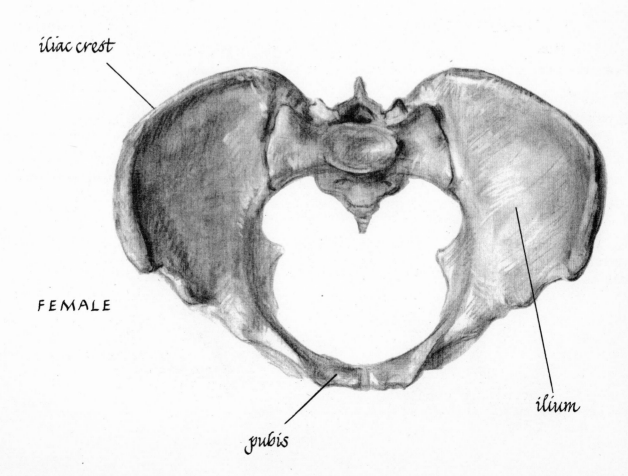

iliac crest

FEMALE

pubis

ilium

Plate 11. PELVIS, FROM SIDE

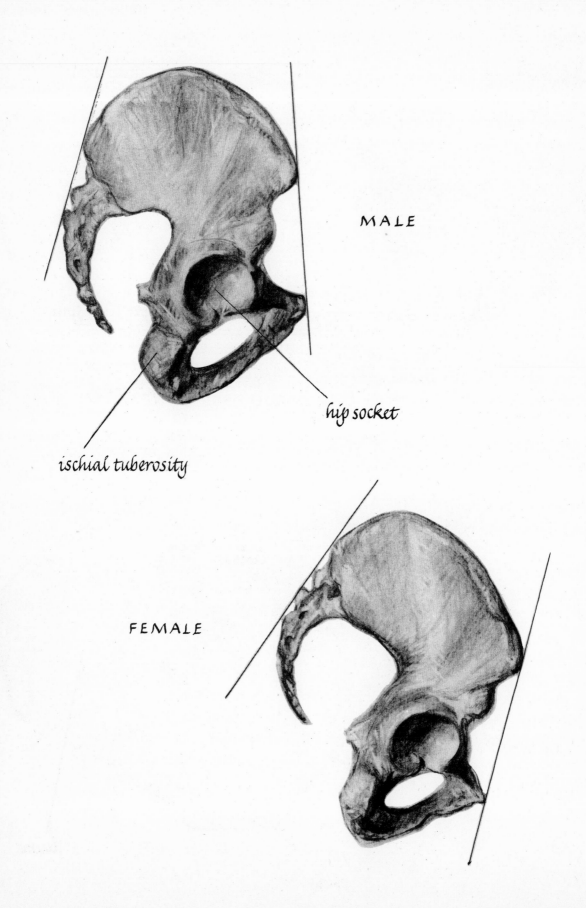

MALE

hip socket

ischial tuberosity

FEMALE

the pubic bones, gives the simplest expression of the mass. This distinct type of pelvis is a human characteristic.

Located at the middle of the body, the pelvis gives attachment to muscles that radiate from it in different directions. From the ilium, crests, spines, pubis, ischium, and sacrum, they run upward onto the rib cage and armbone and downward over the hips and thighs and to the leg.

The *crest of the iliac bones* is subcutaneous and so must be watched for, in locating significant points on the figure for construction.

In the male, the iliac crest is strongly marked by the attachment of the heavy muscular mass above, but it is characteristically more obscure in the female, as the region is absorbed by the plane of the flank starting at the base of the rib cage (page 134).

The *pubis* is another subcutaneous part.

The mass of the *ischium* takes a general direction opposed to that of the ilium. Their relationship is somewhat like that of the two blades of a propeller. Of the ischium, the projecting tuberosity at the back alone affects the surface appearance. These *ischial tuberosities* are sturdily built, to support the weight of the body in the sitting position and to give origin to heavy muscles forming the back of the thigh. The tuberosities become subcutaneous when the thigh is flexed on the trunk, and the hip muscles slip over them.

More than any other part of the skeleton, the pelvis exhibits those distinguishing characteristics which belong to the particular type—male or female. Taken as a whole, the pelvis of the female is broad and shallow compared with that of the male, and this fact accounts for the greater width through the hips so typical of the female figure. But it is not only this increased width that distinguishes the type. Equally significant is the *tilt* of the pelvis. The drawing from profile shows the relative degree of this tilt in the two types. In the male, the upper spine of the iliac crest is immediately over or a little in back of the pubis, while a similar line drawn on the female pelvis slants definitely backward. Thus on the female, the hips are actually set at a slant, while those of the male have practically a vertical axis.

The pitch of the pelvis is determined by a short ligament, which

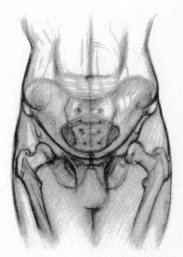

The iliac crests
are subcutaneous

Relation of the pelvis
to the hip mass,
from the front

Pelves of male & female show
characteristic differences

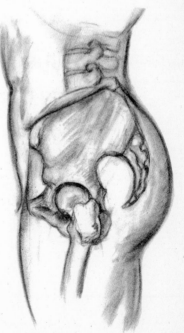

Relation of the pelvis
to the hip mass, from the side

Plate 12. PELVIS & ITS ARTICULATION WITH THE FEMUR

MALE

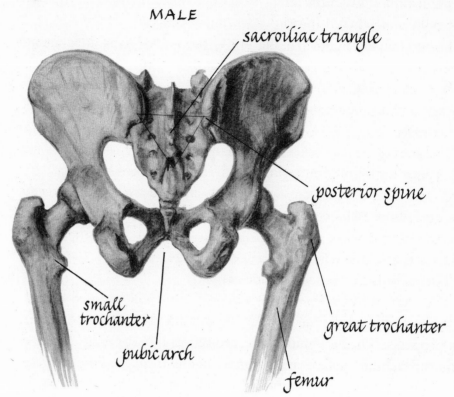

sacroiliac triangle

posterior spine

small trochanter

pubic arch

great trochanter

femur

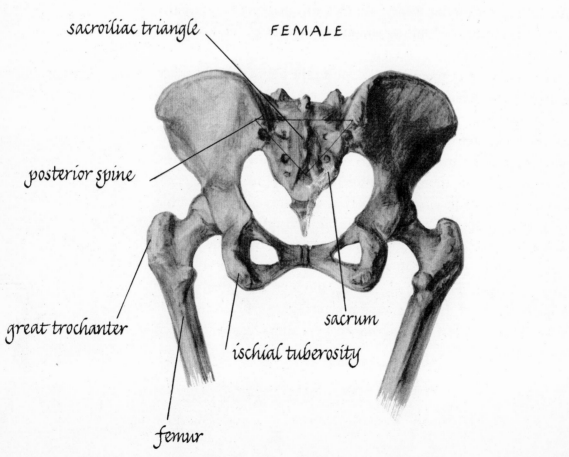

sacroiliac triangle

FEMALE

posterior spine

great trochanter

ischial tuberosity

sacrum

femur

51

runs from the lower iliac spine to the upper end of the shaft of the thighbone and is called the *iliofemoral*, or *Y*, ligament. This ligament is shorter in the female than in the male and so holds down the upper front part of the pelvis, causing its forward pitch.

Accompanying the wider hip bones in the female is the broader sacrum, which increases the separation between the iliac bones; so the *posterior spines* are spaced more widely apart in the female. On the well-developed figure, these spines are conspicuous as dimples and, taken with the prominence at the lowest spine of the sacrum, they form a landmark, known as the *sacroiliac triangle* (pages 132 and 133). This triangle, accordingly, is more acute in the male and more obtuse in the female. Associated with the broadened forms in the female pelvis are the larger opening between the iliac bones and the larger angle of the female *pubic arch*, shown in the comparative drawings (Plate 12).

In the pelvis, the *hip socket,* for reception of the head of the thighbone, is deeper than the socket at the shoulder, for the armbone, and it holds the thighbone more snugly; for, while the arm demands free movement in all directions, the leg is called upon to support and to move the body. So, at the hip socket, while the degree of movement is lessened, strength and stability are increased.

CONSTRUCTION OF THE TRUNK. Viewed from front or back, the trunk is built upon two trapezoid forms, one in-

The iliofemoral, or Y, ligament is shorter in the female than in the male

The trunk is built upon two trapezoid forms

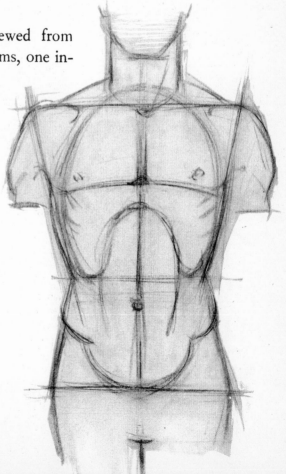

verted upon the other. This gives the simple block effect of the form. Within the upper form fits the rib cage.

In the front, the curves of the rib cartilages and the abdomen supply their constructive form, and the plane of the chest squares the upper part. These squares are beveled above by the shoulder forms. The sternum deepens the midline of the chest, and the subcutaneous iliac crest marks the hip. The clavicles go straight across the shoulders.

In back, the column, the thorax, and the hips are the basic forms. Subcutaneous parts of vertebrae and scapulae, iliac crests, and the sacroiliac triangle determine the placing of the masses. Over the oval of the rib cage, triangular shapes predominate in the back. The length of the scapula is about the same as the distance from the midline on the column to the end of the clavicle, or about half the distance from the seventh cervical vertebra to the waistline. In the normal position, the distance between the scapulae is about a neck's width. There are about three neck widths through the heads of the armbones (Plates 1 and 2 and page 122).

The divisions in the back are important

Construction of the trunk, back

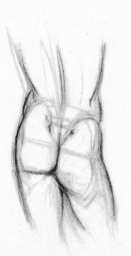

The profile is the most active view, as the masses are eccentrically balanced one above another and produce a dynamic effect. Therefore, the relative directions of the masses are the first consideration. The axes of the head and the rib cage slant forward in descending; that of the pelvis opposes them by running backward, as does the axis of the neck.

From the side, the greatest width of the trunk is not much more than half the maximum width through the shoulders in front view.

Ovals of the rib cage and the hips suggest these masses. The front line of the trunk is a simple sweep, but the line of the back exhibits the four characteristic curves, modified by the shoulder blade. Main cross lines are at neck, chest, rib cartilages, and iliac crest.

The profile is the most active view

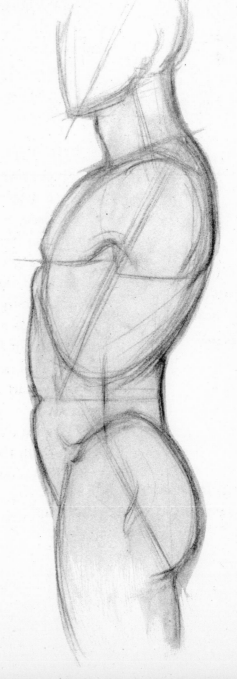

Construction of the trunk, side

THE LOWER LIMB

Ability to bring thigh
in line with trunk is
a human characteristic

Man is distinguished by the ability to bring the lower limb in line with the trunk, an ability not equalled in degree by any creature of similar skeletal structure.

All the bones of the upper and lower limb, with the exception of those of the wrist and the ankle, are long bones, each having a shaft and two prominent extremities. In the lower limb, the portion from the hip joint to the knee will be referred to as the *thigh* and that from knee to ankle, as the *leg*. This follows the common anatomical terminology.

The femur is the
longest bone in the body

THE THIGHBONE. The longest and strongest bone in the body is the *femur*, or thighbone. Its long, round shaft is curved forward and determines the arch of the thigh.

The *head*, by which the femur articulates with the pelvis, is separated from its shaft by a *neck*, which juts upward at an angle of about 125 degrees. This long neck greatly increases the mobility of the femur at the hip joint, and it is a distinct characteristic of the human anatomy.

The long neck
of the femur
gives unique mobility
to the limb

At the outer, upper extremity of the bone is a large prominence, roughened for the attachment of muscle and called the *great trochanter*. This prominence is important on the surface, for it marks the widest part of the hips and also the point halfway down on the figure.

The great trochanter appears as a prominence only when the thigh is bent. With the thigh extended, a depression indicates its location. Other provisions made for the attachment of muscle are the *small*

The great trochanter
is prominent in the bent thigh

54

Plate 13. FEMUR OR THIGHBONE

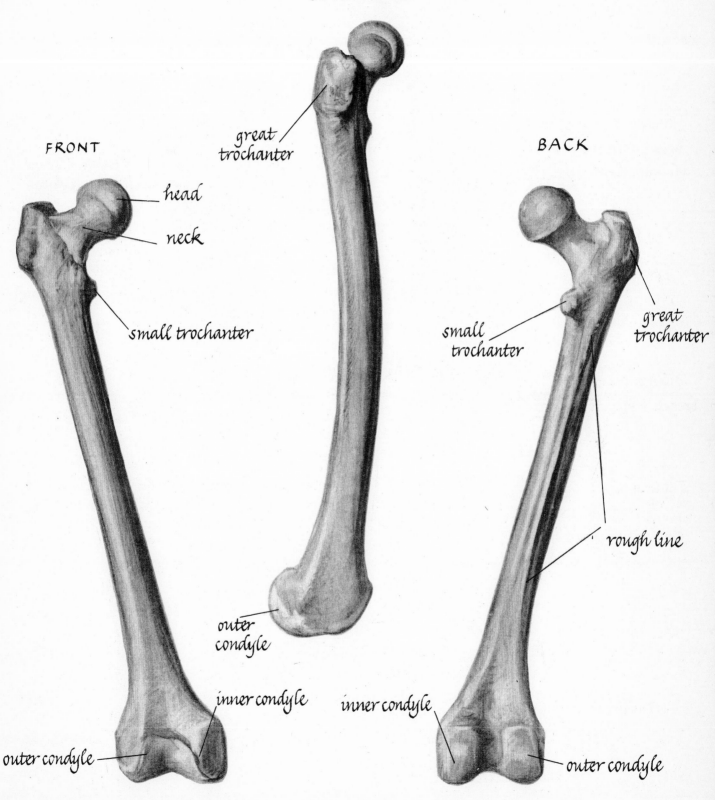

OUTER SIDE

FRONT

BACK

great
trochanter

head

neck

small trochanter

small
trochanter

great
trochanter

rough line

outer
condyle

inner condyle

inner condyle

outer condyle

outer condyle

Plate 14. LEGBONES

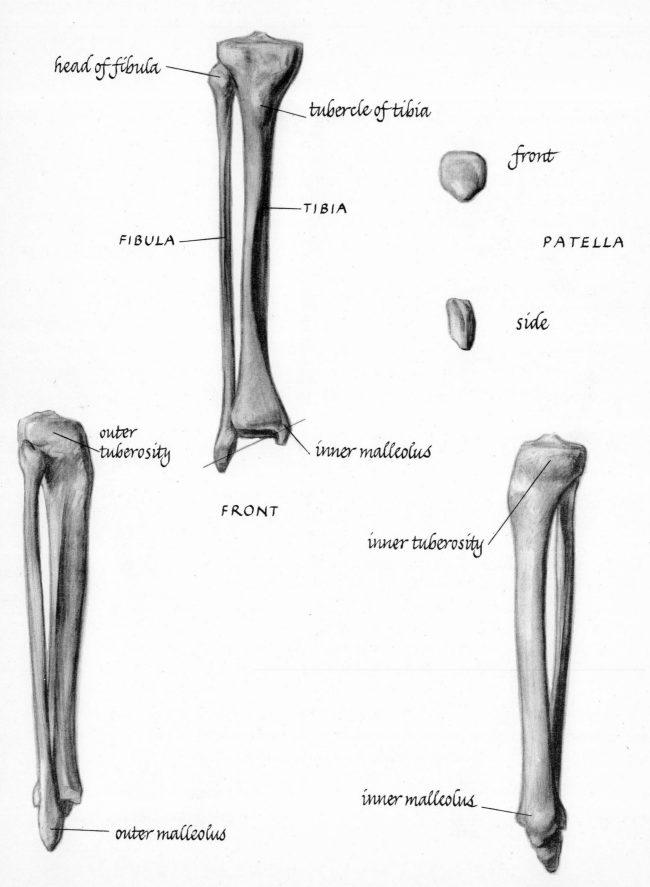

head of fibula

tubercle of tibia

front

TIBIA

PATELLA

FIBULA

side

outer tuberosity

inner malleolus

FRONT

inner tuberosity

outer malleolus

inner malleolus

OUTER SIDE

INNER SIDE

trochanter, which is on the inner side of the femur just below the neck, and the rough ridge on the back of the bone, extending down nearly its whole length. This ridge is called the *linea aspera* ("rough line").

At its lower extremity the femur broadens, forming two large *condyles*, which are smooth and rounded to articulate with the tibia, or shinbone. Between the condyles in front is a depression for the *patella*, or kneecap, and in back this becomes a deep groove as the knoblike condyles project. A projecting wedge on the articular surface of the shinbone fits into this groove, providing attachment for cross ligaments, which, with other ligaments, firmly tie the bones together. The condyles are flattened at the sides, giving the characteristic squareness to the knee. This is especially noticeable at the outer side, the inner condyle being more rounded, as well as more prominent.

In the drawings, the femurs are given the inclination that they have in life. The shaft runs at an angle to the condyles. As the hip sockets are removed farther apart in the wider female pelvis, the thighbones must converge more sharply as they descend to the knees. This extra convergence is definitely a female characteristic (Plates 2 and 12).

The relationships of the forms of the lower limb can readily be seen on one's own figure by looking down the outer side of the leg while standing with the feet well apart. Notice the setback of the knee and the calf and the bracing of the leg against the thigh.

The shaft of the femur is encased in the powerful muscles of the thigh, so that only the great trochanter and the condyles are subcutaneous.

THE BONES OF THE LEG. In the leg are two bones: the *tibia*, or shinbone, and the *fibula*, a long slender bone along the outer side.

The tibia. The upper part of the tibia has two *tuberosities*, which articulate with the condyles of the femur to form the knee joint. In the front, just below the tuberosities, is a prominence called the *tu-*

The condyles cause the squareness & beveling of the knee

The shaft of the femur runs at an angle to the condyles

The convergence of the femurs is more pronounced in the female

Only the great trochanter & the condyles are subcutaneous

The subcutaneous tubercle is prominent on the tibia

bercle of the tibia. This is the point of attachment of the ligament that carries the kneecap.

The inner tuberosity rounds under gently, curving into the inner surface of the shaft. It is more prominent than the outer and continues the rounded form of the condyle above. The shaft of the tibia is triangular in section and is the basis for the triangular character of the calf. At its base, the tibia flares out, forming the rounded prominence of the inner ankle. This prominence is called the *inner malleolus*. In the side view, the tibia slants forward to the tubercle, then takes a reverse curve, convex above and concave at the ankle.

The under surface of the tibia provides articulation with the anklebones.

The tibia is subcutaneous at the tuberosities, the inner malleolus, and along the entire length of the inner plane of its shaft, from inner tuberosity to inner malleolus. This subcutaneous shin plane is important as a structural line on the figure.

The fibula. The fibula fits along the outer side of the tibia, well to the back, and is placed on a lower level than the tibia. Its upper extremity, or *head*, fits against the under surface of the outer tuberosity of the tibia (which brings it below the knee joint). The bone turns upon itself, so that its front above becomes its back below. Ridges run down the bone to give firm lodgment to muscles. There is no movement between the fibula and the tibia.

The lower extremity of the fibula is called the *outer malleolus*. It extends lower and is slightly farther back than the inner malleolus. The outer malleolus is the more prominent of the two. The difference in level of the two prominences gives rise to the characteristic downward and outward slant of the ankle. A study of the three drawings will make clear these important relationships. The fibula is largely embedded in the outer muscles of the leg. Only its head, lower third of shaft, and outer malleolus are subcutaneous.

THE PATELLA. The kneecap, or patella, is a shell-shaped bone, slightly convex forward. It makes the transition between the thigh muscles and the tibia. As its lower limit corresponds to the

The entire inner side of the tibia is subcutaneous

The bone relations at the ankle determine its character

The head & lower third of the fibula are subcutaneous

The patella lies wholly ABOVE the knee joint

Plate 15. KNEE JOINT

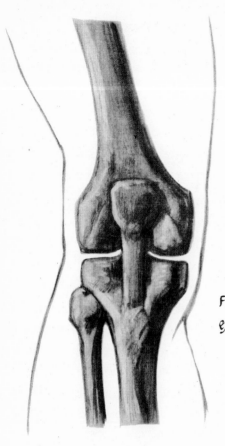

FRONT,
extended

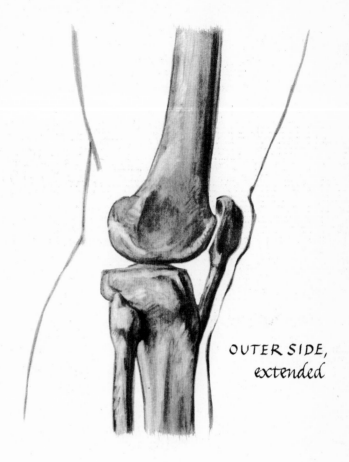

OUTER SIDE,
extended

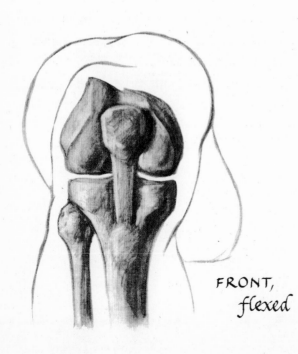

FRONT,
flexed

OUTER SIDE,
flexed

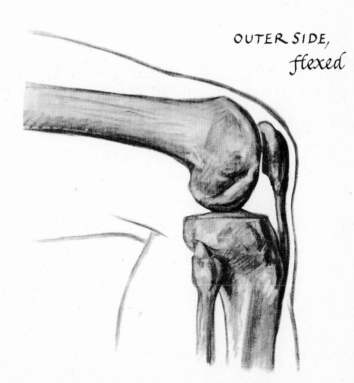

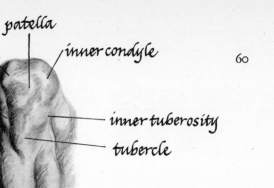

patella
outer condyle
inner condyle
outer tuberosity
inner tuberosity
tubercle

FLEXED

The knee from front,
EXTENDED

In flexion of the knee,
the condyles are exposed

The inner condyle is rounded

When flexed,
the leg appears LONGER
than when extended

The knee from inner side,
EXTENDED

line of the knee joint, the patella is high on the knee and appears as a subcutaneous prominence.

THE KNEE JOINT. The relations of the bones at the knee joint are shown in Plate 16. It will be noted that, in flexing, the tibia moves over the condyles of the femur, or vice versa, depending upon which is fixed. So when the knee is bent at right angles or more, the ends of the condyles are exposed.

In the drawings, the square character of the knee is evident. From the front and in the flexed position, the outer condyle is especially square. The inner side is rounded and the patella is seen to sink into the depression between the condyles.

When the knee is bent, the leg appears longer than in the extended position, the condyles adding their depth to the leg. The leg bone itself extends up only about to the under line of the knee.

From the front, the femur, because of its inclination, meets the tibia at an angle. From the side, the convex line of the femur extends farther forward than the line of the tibia (page 64).

Joints, such as those of knee, ankle, elbow, and wrist, need careful study, as the bones of these regions are subcutaneous and constitute the foundational form.

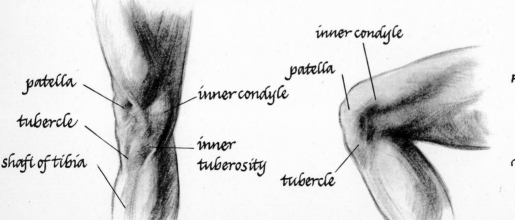

patella
tubercle
shaft of tibia
inner condyle
inner tuberosity

inner condyle
patella
FLEXED
tubercle

The surface effect of bones
is strong at joints

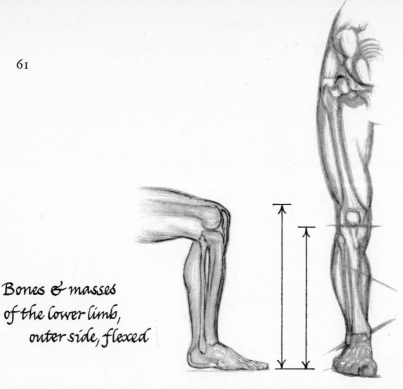

Bones & masses
of the lower limb,
outer side, flexed

Bones & masses
of the lower limb,
front, extended

THE BONES OF THE FOOT. The skeleton of the foot consists of three sets of bones: tarsals, metatarsals, and phalanges.

The seven *tarsals*, or anklebones, comprise the back half of the length of the foot as illustrated in the views of the bones from above or from the inner side. Connecting these with the bones of the toes are the five *metatarsals* (*meta*, "beyond"—beyond the tarsals). The toes each have three *phalanges* (*phalanx*, "ranks of soldiers"), except the great toe, which has two.

Articulation with the tibia and the fibula is through the *talus*, or anklebone, which is provided with a cylindrically curved surface, to fit up into the notch between inner and outer malleoli. The joint so formed permits free action: flexion, extension, and some side-to-side movement.

Under the talus, and supporting it, is the projecting heelbone, the *os calcis*. It bears the weight of the body at the back, forming one of the pillars of the long arch of the foot. In back, on its top is a roughened surface for the attachment of the tendon from calf muscles. Toward its front inner side under the talus, is a projecting shelf for the support of that bone. This can be seen in the drawings of the back and inner side of the bones of the foot.

In front of the talus and the os calcis are grouped the other tarsals:

The bones at the ankle
are designed for
support & locomotion

Plate 16. BONES OF THE FOOT & ANKLE JOINT

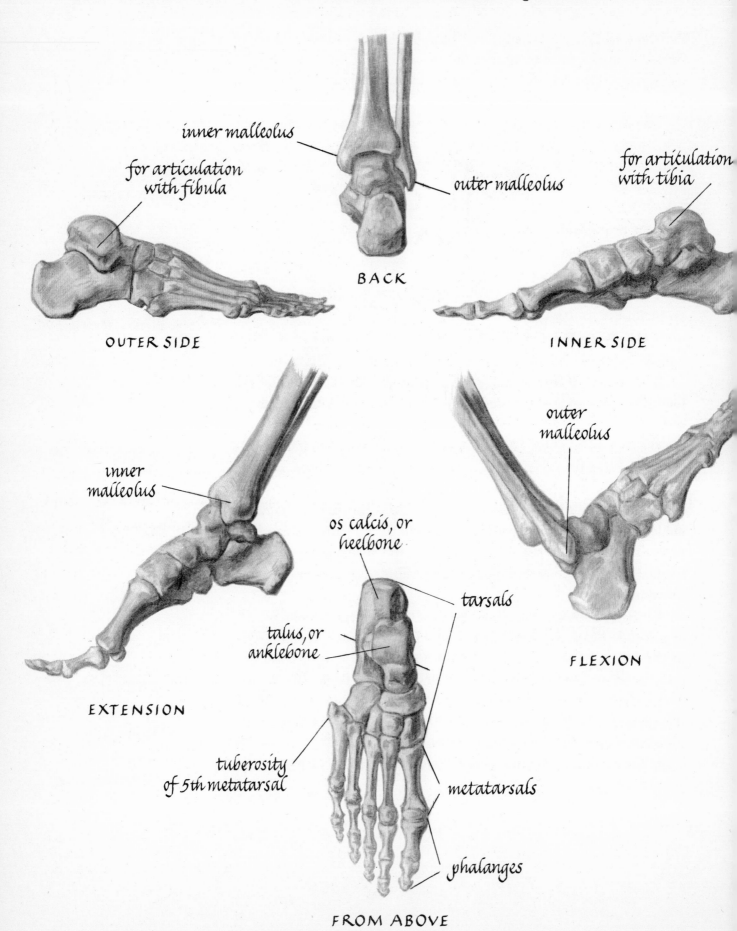

inner malleolus

for articulation with fibula

outer malleolus

BACK

for articulation with tibia

OUTER SIDE

INNER SIDE

inner malleolus

outer malleolus

os calcis, or heelbone

tarsals

talus, or anklebone

FLEXION

EXTENSION

tuberosity of 5th metatarsal

metatarsals

phalanges

FROM ABOVE

the *scaphoid* ("boat-shaped") and then the first *cuneiform* ("wedge-shaped") bones, on the inside; the *cuboid*, to the outside; and the second and third *cuneiforms*, between. These articulate with the five metatarsals and form the arch of the foot.

The five metatarsals have rounded, knoblike lower ends, for articulation with the phalanges. The metatarsal of the second toe is the longest and it wedges between the cuneiforms on either side. In its articulation with the second cuneiform, it makes the apex of the arch of the instep. The first, or metatarsal of the big toe, completes the arch. Its articulation with its phalanx marks the location of the ball of the foot.

On the outer side, the fifth metatarsal has a *tuberosity* for the attachment of tendons from leg muscles. This tuberosity is a landmark on the foot, occurring halfway from the heel to little toe. Just in back of the tuberosity is a groove in the cuboid bone, for the tendon of the long peroneus muscle.

In type, the phalanges are long bones with extremities broader than their shafts. The upper ends of the first phalanges are concave and articulate with the convex terminals of the metatarsals. The terminal phalanx is tipped by a form like an arrowhead, which carries the nail. The phalanges of the toes are much shorter than those of the fingers. In the hand, the phalanges constitute half the total length, but in the foot, much less. The big toe is about one-fourth the length of the entire foot. The second toe is not always the longest, but a more symmetrical foot results when it is so drawn. The ancient Greek sculptors made the second longer than the big toe, as representing the ideal foot.

The proportions of corresponding bones of foot and hand vary in accordance with their differing functions. The fingers are required to perform infinitely varied manipulations, including grasping. The toes, however, are merely the terminals of an instrument of support and progression. As the tarsals bear the weight of the body, they need to be far stronger than their counterparts in the wrist. In the normal position, the foot is at right angles to the axis of the ankle, while the axis of the hand is continuous with that of the wrist.

The tarsals & metatarsals form the arch of the foot

The tuberosity of the fifth metatarsal marks the mid-point between heel & little toe

The phalanges are less important in the foot than in the hand

The foot OPPOSES the ankle, while the hand is CONTINUOUS with the wrist

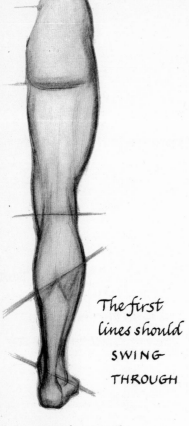

*The first
lines should
SWING
THROUGH*

*Construction of the
lower limb, back*

In the back view, the relation of the malleoli is shown—the inner high, the outer low. Note also, in the view from above, the line marking the relation of the malleoli from front to back, the outer malleolus being farther to the rear than is the inner.

The inner view exhibits the arch. The bones on the outerside extend more in a straight line. When the foot is extended, the instep is more or less in line with the leg, but in the flexed position the angle is less than a right angle.

CONSTRUCTION OF THE LOWER LIMB. From front or back, two converging lines will place the limb—establish its simple direction and length. Sweep in these two lines first. They give the effect of the limb as a whole, and upon them the smaller forms can be developed. The thigh is cylindrical, the knee is cubical, and the leg is triangular in section.

Carrying the form are the subcutaneous parts: the upper iliac spine, the pubis, and the great trochanter at the hip; condyles, tuberosities, tubercle, and patella making the knee; while the shaft of the tibia and malleoli determine the leg and the ankle. From the back the sacroiliac triangle and the os calcis are important.

In profile, the lower limb takes a reverse curve at the front. This is the result of the bend of the femur and the stepping back of the knee. Supporting this simple sweep are the varied directions of the back boundaries. Hip, calf, and heel are prominences, with straight lines connecting. Avoid any break in the swing of the form. From the outer side, the subcutaneous head of the fibula appears at the knee. The outer malleolus at the ankle, and the tubercle of the fifth metatarsal at the foot.

From the inner side, the condyle of the femur, the tuberosity, shaft, and malleolus of the tibia, with the os calcis and first metatarsal, form the bony framework. The masses reveal exceptional rhythm in this view (page 143).

In long forms, such as limbs, much depends upon getting the *coordinating rhythm*. Contrive to express rhythm by swinging the lines through. Careful relating of the long lines will unify the forms.

*Bones & masses of the
lower limb, outer side*

*Avoid any break
in the sweep of the form*

The subtle contour of the female limb is best suggested by long, sweeping curves. There is often a reverse curve in the outer line of the thigh. This is especially evident in the more mature type.

CONSTRUCTION OF THE FOOT. The problem in foot construction arises from the forward growth of the foot, which necessitates foreshortening, as each part is mortised into the part beyond. As with all form, rhythm plays a strong part in the expression of character in the foot. Any break in the rhythm arrests the movement of the form.

In every view, the general effect of the foot is a triangle of some sort. In constructing the foot, look for the quality of "spring," which characterizes it.

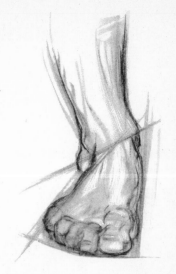

Construction of the foot,
front

The foot is triangular
& has spring

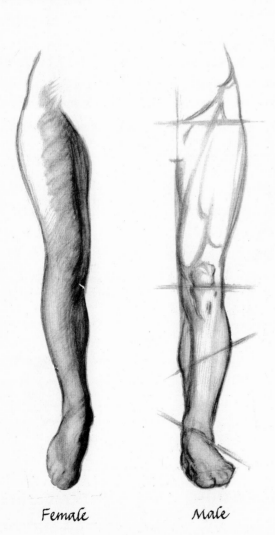

Construction of the foot,
outer side

Female   Male

CONSTRUCTION OF THE LOWER LIMB, FRONT

Plate 17. ARMBONE

BACK

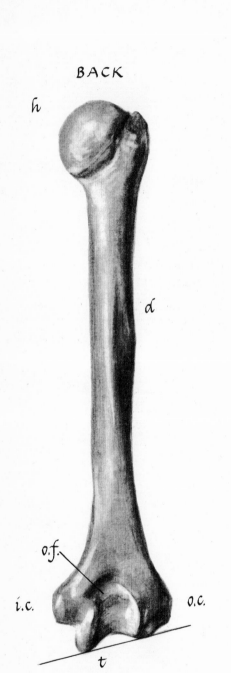

FRONT

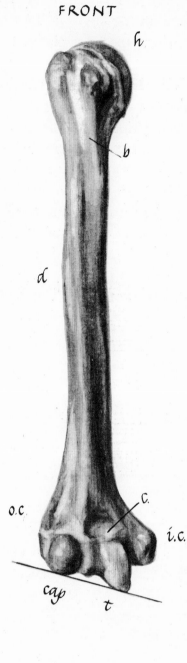

OUTER SIDE

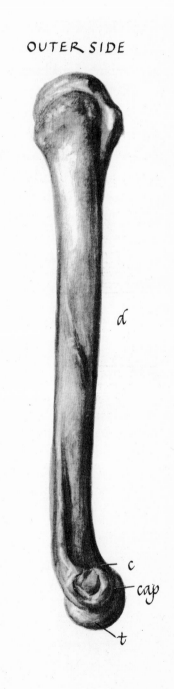

b – BICIPITAL GROOVE

c – CORONOID FOSSA

cap – CAPITELLUM

d – DELTOID IMPRESSION

h – HEAD

i.c. – INNER CONDYLE

o.c. – OUTER CONDYLE

o.f. – OLECRANON FOSSA

t – TROCHLEA

THE UPPER LIMB

In the discussion of these parts, it will simplify the study and will be less confusing to refer to the segment from the shoulder to the elbow as the *arm* and that below the elbow joint as the *forearm*.

The bones of the upper limb are three in number. The humerus is the bone of the arm, while in the forearm are the ulna and the radius. The ulna forms the main part of the elbow joint by hinging on the humerus. The radius forms the main part of the wrist and carries the hand.

THE ARMBONE. The armbone, or *humerus*, has several features that strongly influence the appearance of the arm. Its rounded *head* fundamentally determines the rounded form of the cap of the shoulder. At the other extremity, the bone is broadened and flattened laterally and is triangular in shape. The arm at the elbow is molded on this form. The hemispherical head of the humerus is set obliquely to the shaft. This head forms the articular surface that fits loosely into the *glenoid cavity* of the scapula to form the joint of the shoulder.

The humerus bases the forms of the arm

The free relationship between these surfaces provides the maximum capacity for movement, and that is the prerequisite of the arm. This movement is very great in the glenoid cavity itself, being restricted only by ligaments and by the eventual contact of the armbone with the wall of the cavity. But added to this ability for free movement within the shoulder socket is the provision for auxiliary movement of the whole bladebone, which contains this socket and which we have already noticed. This greatly augments the potentialities of movement at the shoulder.

The shoulder socket is designed for free movement

67

Near the head of the humerus there are *two tuberosities*, which, between them, form a long depression called the *bicipital groove*. This groove is designed to carry one of the long tendons of the biceps muscle and to give attachment to several other muscles that move the arm.

Nearly halfway down the shaft of the humerus is a roughened ridge, known as the *deltoid impression*, because it is the point of insertion of the deltoid muscle, which caps the shoulder.

Like all bones of its type, the humerus has a certain fluency of line, which is itself rhythmic and suggests the activity that characterizes the arm throughout life. There is never anything rigid or static in the line of any bone, but there is a distinct swing in all anatomical form.

The lower extremity of the humerus requires careful study, because of the complicated nature of its articular surfaces, of which it has a greater variety than belongs to any other similar region. The reason for this will be clear when we consider the varied movements that the elbow joint is required to perform.

First, there is the hinge action of the joint by which the forearm is bent upon the arm, as the leg is bent upon the thigh. But besides this, there is the movement of rotation affecting the elbow, by which the hand is turned palm up or palm down. This different type of action necessitates another sort of articular surface.

For the articulation of the humerus with the ulna, a spoollike surface is provided. This is called the *trochlea* ("pulley") and is placed on an angle, so that the inner flange of the pulley is lower than the outer flange. This is important for it means that, in joining the humerus, the ulna cannot lie in a continuous line with the humerus but must fit on it at an angle. This angle is apparent on the subject when the hand is turned palm forward so that the ulna and the radius lie in a parallel relation. In the illustration showing these bones, the natural relation has been maintained and is evident in back and front views.

Placed just outside the trochlear surface on the humerus is the *capitellum* ("little head"), a small, smoothly rounded projection sim-

The humerus has a rhythmic swing suggesting its activity

The elbow joint provides both hinge & rotary movement

The trochlea accounts for the angle at the elbow

ilar in character to the large head at the shoulder end of the bone. The capitellum is provided for articulation with the head of the radius and serves the requirements for both the hinging movement occurring when the elbow is bent and the turning movement occasioned when the radius rotates about the ulna. This action of the radius will be described in greater detail later.

Projections on the humerus at the inner and outer sides of the lower end of the bone are called *condyles*. The *inner condyle* is always subcutaneous and appears as a sharp prominence. The *outer condyle*, which is on a level with its neighbor, more often shows as a depression, because of the muscles that project on each side of it. It is prominent, however, when the elbow is bent.

THE BONES OF THE FOREARM. The two bones of the forearm, *ulna* and *radius*, are opposites in many respects. The ulna is large above and tapers down to its head at the wrist. The radius has its small end, the head, at the top and is large at the lower end. The two bones, however, are about the same size at their middle, as the cross section shows (Plate 22).

As has been pointed out, the ulna is the bone that, with the humerus, forms the hinge of the elbow joint; but it has little to do with the articulation of the wrist. Conversely, the radius has little function in bending the elbow, but it articulates with the carpal bones of the wrist and so bears the hand.

The ulna. For its articulation with the armbone, the ulna has a structure like an open beak, which grasps the trochlea of the humerus and glides over it in bending the elbow. This concave articular surface of the ulna is called the *sigmoid cavity* and is formed by two projecting processes—the *olecranon* above and the *coronoid* below. Incidentally, the olecranon process forms the point of the elbow. Small sunken areas, called *fossae*, are supplied just above the trochlea of the humerus in front and in back. The *coronoid fossa*, lying in front, accommodates the coronoid process of the ulna when the elbow is fully bent. Similarly, in back is the *olecranon fossa*, which receives the tip of the olecranon process when the elbow joint is extended. These

The condyles of the humerus are subcutaneous

The ulna completes the elbow joint, & the radius, the wrist joint

The olecranon process forms the point of the elbow

Plate 18. BONES OF THE FOREARM

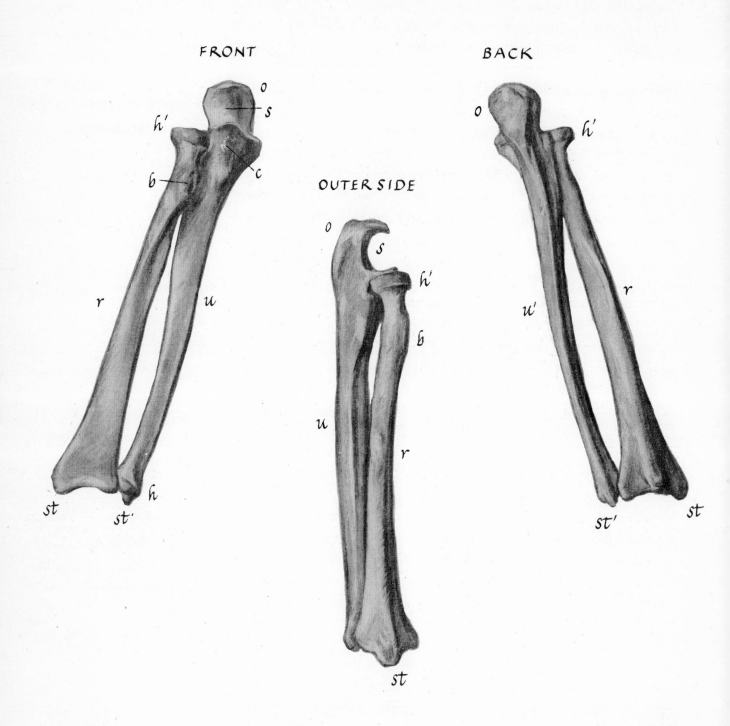

FRONT

BACK

OUTER SIDE

b – BICIPITAL TUBEROSITY

c – CORONOID PROCESS

h – HEAD OF ULNA

h′ – HEAD OF RADIUS

o – OLECRANON PROCESS

r – RADIUS

s – SIGMOID CAVITY

st – STYLOID PROCESS, RADIUS

st′ – STYLOID PROCESS, ULNA

u – ULNA

u′ – ULNAR BORDER

hollows, by receiving the corresponding projections on the ulna, lock the joint, arresting any further movement.

There is a small prominence on the head of the ulna below, called the *styloid process*. The head of the ulna is conspicuous at the back of the wrist on the little finger side. It is smoothly rounded and fits into a corresponding hollow in the radius, so that the radius may move around the ulna, thus rotating the wrist and the hand. Above, a shallow notch is provided on the outside of the coronoid process, in which the head of the radius turns. The drawings opposite explain these relationships.

Like the shaft of the tibia in the leg, the shaft of the ulna is subcutaneous from the point of the elbow all the way to the wrist. It may readily be felt as it forms the division between the flexor muscles on the front and the extensors on the back of the forearm. Its border takes a double curve.

The radius. The *head* of the radius is a thick disk, hollowed out on top for articulation with the capitellum. This construction allows hinge action with rotary movement. In fact, the two movements may be performed simultaneously, the radius moving up or down with the bending of the elbow at the same time that it rotates the wrist.

On the radius, a short distance below the head, is a prominence called the *bicipital tubercle,* from the fact that it forms the point of attachment of the biceps tendon.

Broadening as it descends, the radius attains a width equal to the width of the carpal bones, or wristbones; it has, on its lower end, an articular surface, where it engages the carpals. On the thumb side, its *styloid process* extends downward in a small, pointed knob.

The wrist joint permits side-to-side and rotary, as well as forward and back, movement.

THE ELBOW JOINT. Structure of joints such as those of the elbow and the knee are especially important, because in them the bone form is essentially subcutaneous and has a determining influence upon the appearance; also, because the phases of movement are so considerable and, at the elbow, so complicated.

The head of the ulna is prominent on the little finger side of the wrist. Its articulation with the radius provides for rotation

The shaft of the ulna is subcutaneous from elbow to wrist

The wrist joint permits rotary as well as bending movements

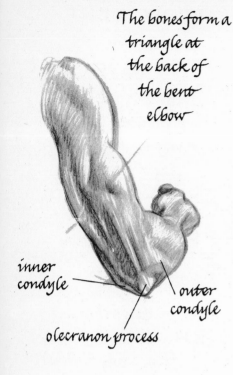

The bones form a triangle at the back of the bent elbow

inner condyle

outer condyle

olecranon process

The relations of the bones to the masses should be studied from different views

The elbow should be studied from various angles and in the extended and flexed positions; then drawings should be done *from memory*. For not until you can visualize the material sufficiently to do this, have you actually made it your own.

In the back view of the bent elbow, an inverted triangle is formed by lines joining the inner and outer condyles and the olecranon. This is characteristic.

The drawings from the outer side, which show the elbow in the extended position and in the two positions of bending, illustrate how the sigmoid cavity is progressively applied to the different parts of the trochlea and carries with it the head of the radius over the capitellum.

In the extended position, movement has been arrested by the locking of the olecranon process in the olecranon fossa on the humerus. In the half-bent position, the contacts are made between the middle portions of the articular surfaces of these bones; while in the fully flexed action, further bending has been limited by the contact of the coronoid process of the ulna with the coronoid fossa of the humerus. The head of the radius is similarly restricted by the hollow above the capitellum.

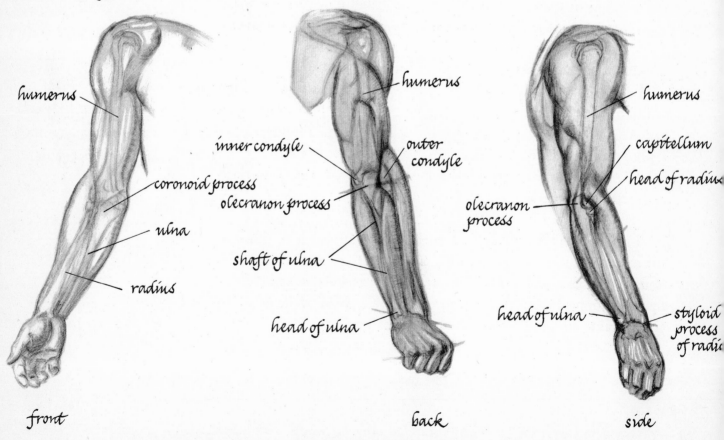

humerus

coronoid process

ulna

radius

inner condyle

outer condyle

olecranon process

shaft of ulna

head of ulna

humerus

humerus

capitellum

head of radius

olecranon process

head of ulna

styloid process of radius

front

back

side

BONES & MASSES OF THE UPPER LIMB

Plate 19. ELBOW JOINT

FRONT

BACK, FLEXED

BACK

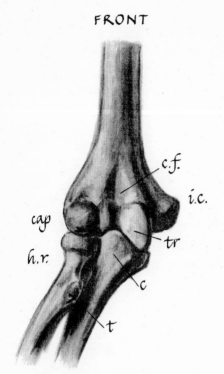
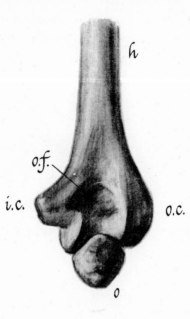
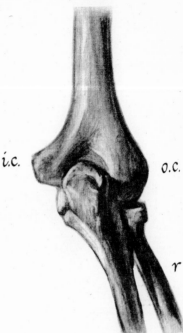

OUTER SIDE

EXTENDED

HALF FLEXED

FULLY FLEXED

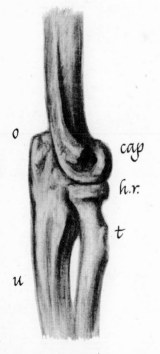
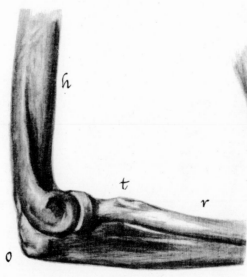
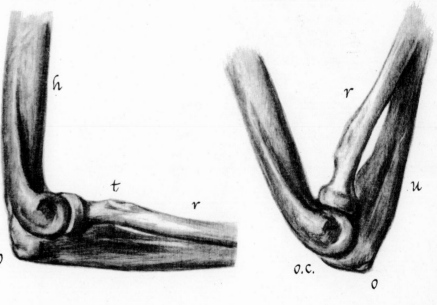

c – CORONOID PROCESS
cap – CAPITELLUM
c.f. – CORONOID FOSSA
h – HUMERUS

h.r. – HEAD OF RADIUS
i.c. – INNER CONDYLE
o – OLECRANON PROCESS
o.c. – OUTER CONDYLE
o.f. – OLECRANON FOSSA

r – RADIUS
t – BICIPITAL TUBEROSITY
tr – TROCHLEA
u – ULNA

Plate 20. BONES OF THE WRIST & PALM

FROM ABOVE

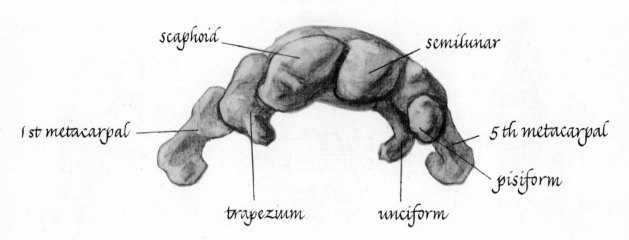

scaphoid

semilunar

1st metacarpal

5th metacarpal

pisiform

trapezium

unciform

PALM

BACK

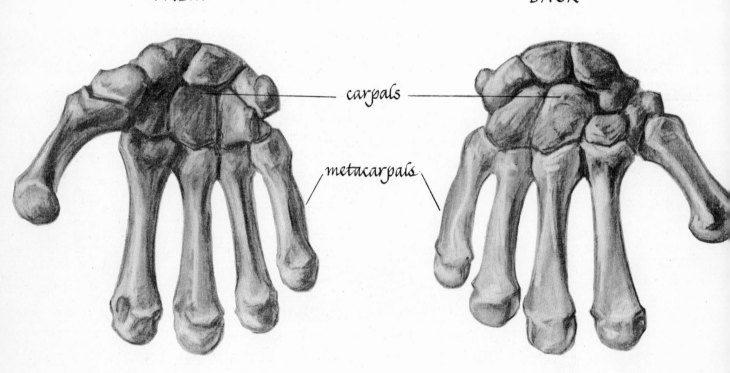

carpals

metacarpals

*The bony structure of the hand
is designed for
infinite uses*

THE BONES OF THE HAND. When we consider its infinite uses, we realize what a wonderful structure the hand is. Its many movable joints give it the greatest flexibility. No part of the body is subject to so extensive a variety of movements. Because of its 27 bones and 16 movable joints, the relations between the various parts of the hand are constantly changing. Unlike the human head, where the relationship of the planes is fundamentally fixed, in the hand the planes may arrange themselves in a great many ways. For example, a view of the back of the hand may or may not show the thumb and the fingers; or any finger may be made to show individually. The thumb and the fingers may be flexed or extended in different degrees, individually or in groups, giving rise to a wide variety of constructions. These are multiplied by every change in the view.

In the hand, the bones are fundamental, as they are subcutaneous across the back surface. Grasping the hand of the skeleton, we sense the basic character of the bones, for the skeleton's hand has much the same "feel" as the living hand.

The skeleton of the hand, like that of the foot, is composed of three groups of bones. They are carpals, or wristbones; metacarpals, or bones of the hand proper; and the phalanges, which form the fingers and thumb.

The carpals. The carpal bones are eight in number, comparable to the seven tarsal bones of the foot. Like the tarsals, they are of irregular shape and are named for their resemblance to certain type forms, as trapezium, semilunar, pisiform, cuneiform, etc. They count as a mass that arches strongly on the back, as shown in Plate 20, leaving a corresponding channel on the palm side. Through this pass the group of tendons from the muscles lodged in the forearm—the flexors of the wrist and those of the fingers.

*The carpals in the upper row from the thumb side
are the scaphoid, semilunar, cuneiform, & pisiform.
In the lower row are the trapezium, trapezoid,
os magnum & unciform*

The carpals connect the forearm
bones with those
of the hand

76

The carpals are arranged, roughly, in two rows, the upper row articulating with the radius and the lower row with the metacarpals of the thumb and the four fingers. The upper ends are convex, to fit into the concave articular end of the radius. Their lower ends are angular and make a jagged line of articulation with the metacarpals. In mass, the carpals appear laid up like a stone wall. The carpals form the transition between the bones of the forearm and those of the hand proper.

In the joints between the individual carpals there is no appreciable movement. However, the joining of the several small carpal units gives elasticity to the mass, reducing rigidity and absorbing shock. The carpals are the only bones in the entire arm that are not of the long type.

The metacarpals. There is a metacarpal bone for each finger and one for the thumb. These form the main part of the body of the hand. They have their shafts flattened on the convex back plane of the hand and rounded on the concave palm surface. Their lower ends are round for articulation with the phalanges and are larger than their upper extremities, so that the hand is heaviest through its middle. When a fist is made, the ends of the metacarpals are exposed as the first phalanx bones glide over them, thus revealing the forms known as the *knuckles* (page 167).

(page 167)

The joint between the thumb carpal (trapezium) and its metacarpal is designed to give the maximum of movement to the thumb. The articular surfaces are described as *saddle-shaped*—a term which graphically expresses the easy movement attained here, a movement that permits apposition of the thumb and the fingers, as in grasping or in holding a small object. This action is not readily possible between fingers alone. Another liberating feature of the thumb is that its metacarpal is not bound to the other metacarpals by ligament. Those for the fingers are thus bound together. The great mobility of the thumb and its *power of opposition* have been strong factors in human development for they have given man the fullest possible use of his hands.

On the back of the hand, where the carpals join the metacarpals,

The metacarpals
make the transition
between the wrist
& finger bones

The joint
at the base of
the thumb
permits free
movement

A change of plane occurs on the back of the hand

Plate 21. BONES OF THE HAND

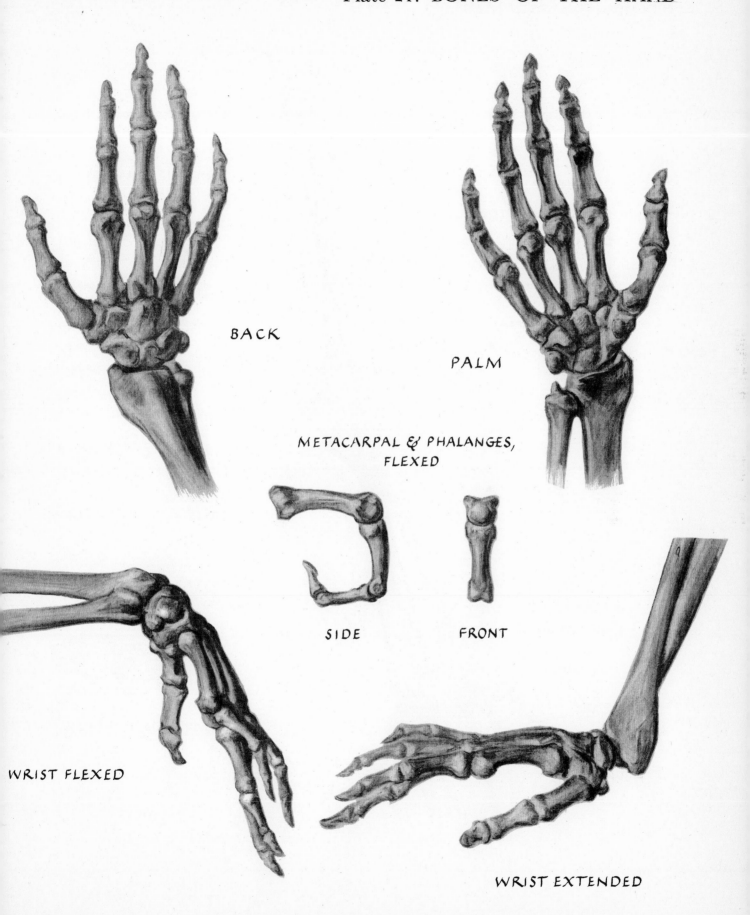

BACK

PALM

METACARPAL & PHALANGES,
FLEXED

SIDE

FRONT

WRIST FLEXED

WRIST EXTENDED

Plate 22. SUPINATION & PRONATION

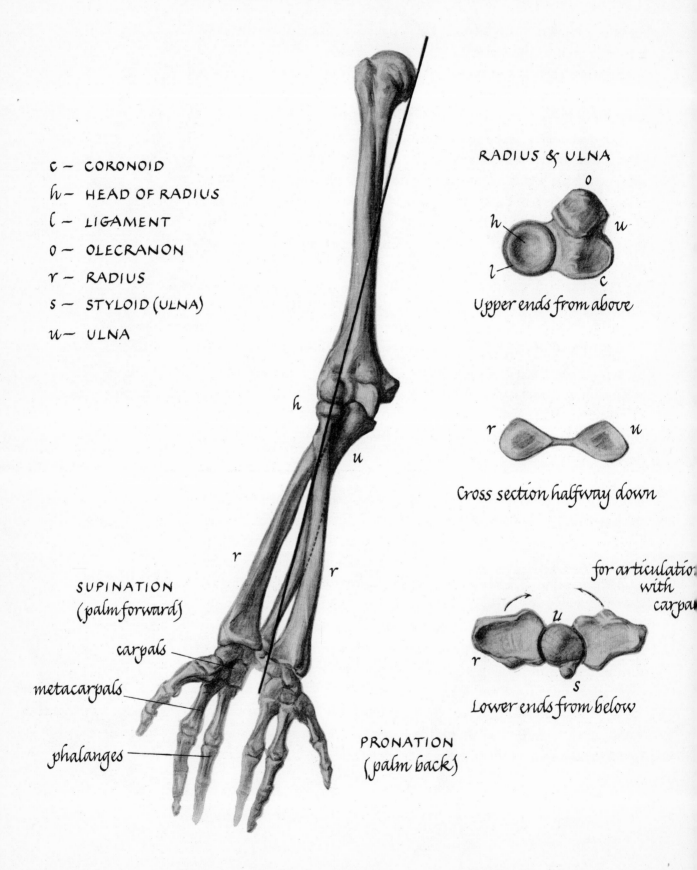

c — CORONOID
h — HEAD OF RADIUS
l — LIGAMENT
o — OLECRANON
r — RADIUS
s — STYLOID (ULNA)
u — ULNA

RADIUS & ULNA

Upper ends from above

Cross section halfway down

SUPINATION
(palm forwards)

carpals

metacarpals

phalanges

PRONATION
(palm backs)

for articulatio
with
carpa

Lower ends from below

there is a marked prominence. This change of plane gives the characteristic arch to the wrist.

Between carpals and metacarpals there is little movement, except at the thumb, though the joints at the third and the little finger have some flexibility.

The phalanges. Each finger has three phalanges and the thumb has two. These bones are convex on the back and flattened on the palm side, where the planes are sharply defined. The phalanges taper downward, and their lower ends are squared like the condyles of the femur. In the middle of the lower end of each segment there is a small groove, into which fits a projection in the segment next below. The last segment is provided with a tip resembling an arrowhead, which carries the nail. The last two joints provide only hinge action, but both hinge and lateral movements are possible at the knuckle joints.

SUPINATION AND PRONATION. The movements by which the hand is turned palm up and palm down are termed *supination* and *pronation*. While the elbow joint remains stationary, the radius merely turns within its orbicular ligament *without altering the relative positions of the bones at the elbow*. This constant relation of the radius and the ulna is shown in the view from above. But in turning on its own axis, the lower end of the radius actually travels halfway around the wrist end of the ulna, thus bringing the hand from the palm up to the palm down position.

The radius carries the hand

The movement is ideally illustrated by the action of a woman slowly wielding a fan. The elbow does not move. It is the radius which is moving about the ulna, turning with it the hand holding the fan. The movement ordinarily is from pronation part way toward supination and back again. The fanning action may habitually proceed at the rate of 50 or more quarter turns per minute. The act of turning a doorknob is another typical example of the movements of supination and pronation.

The position of the upper limb in which the hand is forward or facing up is regarded as the normal position, because here the two forearm bones are in their simplest (parallel) relation. This is referred

In supination, the palm is presented

to as the *position of supination*, for in it the hand is supine, or on its back. In the palm-down position attained after the radius has made its half circuit around the ulna, the shaft of the radius lies across the ulna, for the ulna has remained stationary. The position of the arm in this relation of the bones is called *pronation*, as the hand is prone, or on its face.

When the limb hangs naturally at the side with the palm facing in toward the body, the position of the forearm bones is one that is midway between supination and pronation, as the radius now lies partly across the ulna.

With the limb extended downward in the position of supination, the forearm juts out at an angle to the arm, as has been explained. And if a straight line is drawn from the inner boundary of the head of the humerus to the corresponding part on the head of the ulna, such a line will pass through the middle of the head of the radius. The line, therefore, becomes the axis of revolution of the radius. For comparison, in Plate 22 the supine and prone positions are combined in one drawing. A suggestion of the thumb and the first two fingers is given for each of the two positions. In a drawing of this sort, obviously the remaining fingers could not be included without confusion.

Another composite drawing shows a view of the under sides of the radius and the ulna at the wrist. Here, of course, we are looking into the concave surface of the radius, which furnishes articulation with the carpal bones, or wristbones. The head of the ulna has little direct articulation with the wrist. On the left of the ulna, the radius is shown in the position of supination and, on the right, it has made the half revolution about the ulna to the prone position.

In the movement from supination to pronation, the wrist may make a half-circle turn. This can be demonstrated by turning the wrist while the forearm is bent at right angles to the arm. Now if the

In pronation, the back of the hand is presented

In supination, the angle at the elbow is prominent

Forearm & hand in position of PRONATION (left) & SUPINATION (right)

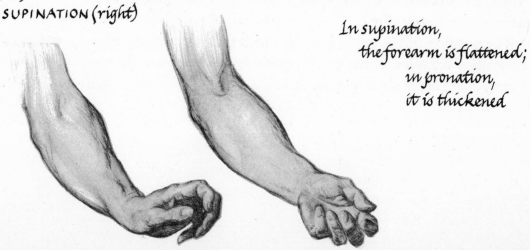

In supination, the forearm is flattened; in pronation, it is thickened

limb is extended at the elbow and the arm is pronated, it will be found that the rotation of the limb can be continued nearly through the full circle. Rotation of the humerus in the shoulder socket accounts for the additional movement.

The two movements occasion changes in the form of the forearm. In the position of supination, where the radius and the ulna are parallel, the upper forearm is flattened—broader than it is deep. But as the radius crosses the ulna, it displaces the muscular mass, so that in the position of pronation the forearm is thicker than it is wide.

HAND CONSTRUCTION. The hand is anatomically unique. As the executive instrument of the individual, it is most versatile in its functions. It is capable of doing the bidding of the steelworker or the violinist; the surgeon or the pugilist.

It, therefore, has innumerable aspects, depending first upon its state: whether it is relaxed or whether the fingers are extended or flexed and to whatever extent. If it is in action, there is the question of the degree and the kind of action.

The hand has innumerable aspects

Then there is the matter of type; and here is the same infinite variety as is found in heads. Age, race, sex, and occupation are determinant factors.

Because of these complications, simple methods of construction are especially desirable. One always has a convenient model in one's own hand, which should be studied directly or from the mirror in all possible positions.

The transverse arcs connecting the joints establish the relations in the hand

As the hand is not a symmetrical form, each view presents a different problem in construction.

But this does not imply that it is more difficult to draw than are other parts; for, once the principles of its construction are understood, the hand may readily be drawn.

In any position, the lines connecting the joints (the points where changes of plane originate) swing in curves, delicately increasing in degree toward the ends of the fingers. These related, curving lines are

Construction of the hand, dorsal side

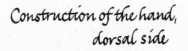

Construction of the hand,
palm side

In profile,
the hand shows a drop
from one segment
to the one next below

essential in maintaining the unified character of the hand. And there is also a convergence of the fingers toward the central axis.

A rhythmic variation occurs in the lengths of the individual segments of the phalanges, as they grow progressively shorter toward the ends of the fingers. Each is two-thirds as long as the one nearer the wrist. This may be observed in the back view of the hand.

In the palm view, the creases divide the fingers more equally, though the third, or end, segment is often the longest, while the middle segment is the shortest division on the fingers. On the palm side, too, the first and third segments are rounded and the middle one is flat. Three skin pads occur on the palm, falling in line with the three divisions between the fingers.

The side view reveals a drop at the joint from one segment to the one below. The relations of the creases to the finger joints may also be compared in this view.

Taking proportions on the hand in life, the middle finger is the longest and measures over half the length of the hand. The thumb reaches nearly to the middle joint of the index finger, and the index finger reaches half way down the terminal segment of the middle finger. The little finger extends about to the last joint of the third finger.

Details, such as creases and nails, need to be suggested very lightly, lest they destroy the main form. It is this form that dominates and that furnishes the strong accents. Fingernails do not supersede the basic form, but merely mean a change in plane and texture at the fingertips.

COMPARISON OF FINGERS AND TOES. As a group, the fingers are longer than the toes, but the big toe is usually longer and sturdier than the thumb. Because of its part in supporting the weight, the big toe is as long as—often longer than—the other toes; but in the hand, the fingers exceed the thumb in length. The thumb is short and powerful—shorter than the little finger on the dorsal side. The planes can best be observed when the arm is extended horizontally toward the light.

CONSTRUCTION OF THE UPPER LIMB. Place the whole limb at once with two converging lines. These should go through—into the fingers. Cross lines may then be put in to mark elbow and wrist joints and the widest part of the arm, near the armpit.

In either front or back views, the inner line makes a simple sweep, requiring little modification; but on the outer side there is a succession of bulging forms, those at the shoulder and the upper forearm being the most prominent. A lesser fullness occurs just above the wrist on the thumb side (Plate 46).

The lines down through the forearm and the wrist determine the index and middle fingers. These, opposed by the thumb, dominate the hand. The other fingers are drawn in relation to them.

The lines should SWING THROUGH into the fingers

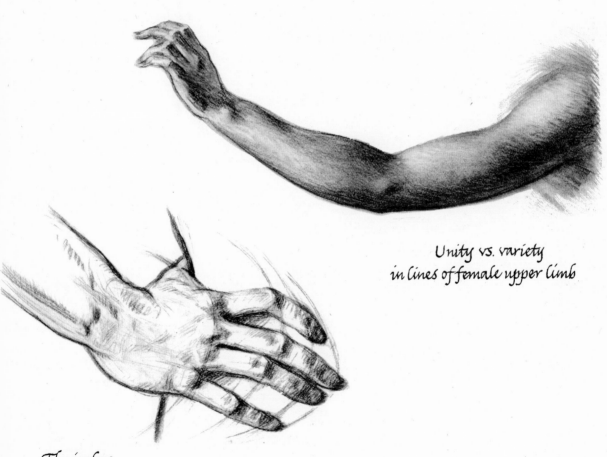

Unity vs. variety in lines of female upper limb

The index & middle fingers dominate the hand

PART II

The true nature of the living muscular
structure — how it determines the masses
& moves the figure — what to look for; &
how to express the character of the forms.

THE MUSCLES

From our earlier study, we have gained an idea of the basic character of the skeleton in its effect upon the outward human form. We have also considered the relation of the bones to this form and have examined the character of the main masses of the figure.

In further developing the subject, we shall inquire into those forces which move the body and which comprise the muscular system.

This study will provide a more complete understanding of the fundamental structure and its appearance when active, as well as when in the relaxed state.

The plates show the muscles as they *actually are,* while the construction drawings show how they *appear*—how they affect the form.

Like most natural, living forms, the human figure is symmetrical, and there are two of each of the muscles—one on each side of the axis. Those muscles bordering on either the front or the back axis, naturally have their two parts reversed at the axis, like the two sides of a leaf or of a butterfly.

In the front, the axis is the line from the pit of the neck to the pubis. In the back, the axis of the trunk is the spinal column.

The skeleton furnishes the only fixed masses in the figure. The muscles follow this framework, emphasizing its forms. They reinforce and develop the structure. Since the muscles give form and movement to the figure, an accurate knowledge of each important muscle, of its location, and of how it acts, is essential to a complete comprehension of the form. Mere mapping of the muscles is misleading, for muscles do not appear on the surface with fixed and con-

The color plates show the muscles as they actually are. The construction drawings show how the muscles appear on the form

The facts about muscles need to be understood by the artist

tinuous boundary lines. To understand the effect of muscles and to express them, one must learn what to look for. There is no other way. We must find out where and how a muscle appears under various conditions. The covering of the outer skin, together with any incidental subcutaneous fatty tissue, obscures in some degree the separation of muscles, and their appearance changes with every movement. This renders the effect subtle; but with a practical understanding of the structure we shall know what to look for.

Muscle is composed of contractile tissue. Growing out of the bone, it crosses over one or more joints and is attached to another bone. Muscles work on the principle of the lever. From its point of origin, a muscle acts upon the part where it is inserted; *i.e.,* from a more or less fixed point it acts upon a free part. By its contraction, or shortening, the muscle draws the free part toward the fixed part. If the muscle passes over the front of the joint, it bends, or flexes, the joint. Such muscles are often named *flexors*. If the muscle crosses the back of a joint, it straightens, or extends, that joint. These muscles are usually termed *extensors*. Thus muscles are sometimes named for their *functions: adductor, tensor, supinator*. They are also classified according to their *appearance: teres* ("round"), *deltoid* ("triangular"), *gracilis* ("slender"), *biceps* ("two-headed"), etc. Some are named from their *location: sternomastoid* (sternum to mastoid process), *pectoralis* (chest), *tibialis* (shin).

A muscle is said to be *superficial* wherever it is not covered by other muscular structure. The *deep* muscles are those underneath the superficial ones. For our purpose, it is essential to know about 66 muscles.

There are three facts that should be known about a muscle. Obviously the first is its *appearance*—its shape and relative size. Next comes its *location* and extent—where it starts and where it is inserted. The third is its function—what its *action* is.

Muscle has three phases that determine its physical appearance: relaxed, contracted, and stretched.

From the relaxed condition, a muscle shortens and becomes more prominent when acting. It is drawn out or flattened when stretched.

Muscles work on the principle of the lever

The appearance, location, & action of each muscle need to be known

The appearance of a muscle is dependent upon its state, whether relaxed, contracted, or stretched

Muscles of the face and the trunk, especially, have quite different appearance themselves in these different states and, consequently, may cause radical changes in the appearance of those parts of the figure where they occur. A contraction on one side of the trunk causes stretching on the other side, and this results in variety and unity.

Muscles are of generally convex form, their greatest thickness usually being near their middle. Therefore, *anatomical form in general is convex* and its representation is strengthened by careful attention to this fact. A common fault is the hollowing out of forms.

The Herculean type ideally exemplifies the convex nature of the muscles

THE HEAD II

Two superficial muscles assist in mastication. These act in closing the jaw. One occupies the depression at the temple and is called the *temporal*. The other fills out the side of the jaw and is named for its function, the *masseter*. (The muscles that open the jaw are concealed beneath the chin and the jaw, and so are little in evidence.)

THE TEMPORAL MUSCLE. The temporal muscle is fan-shaped. Its fibers converge from along the temporal ridge and are attached to a prominence on the mandible, called the *coronoid process*. Its attachment is hidden by the zygomatic arch.

THE MASSETER MUSCLE. The masseter muscle originates on the under side of the zygomatic arch. It runs obliquely downward and backward to the angle of the jaw, causing considerable modification of the form as it rounds it out.

These muscles can best be studied on the head during the act of chewing. When the mouth is alternately opened and closed, the sliding back and forth of the jawbone at its articulation produces the two conspicuous moving prominences, one at the temple and the other on the jaw. Any eating establishment provides a good laboratory for observing the working of these muscles.

MUSCLES OF THE FACE. Particularly do the muscles of the face and the neck require simplification. In all their intricate detail, these present so formidable an aspect as to fill with dread even the most earnest art student. Though they are scientifically interest-

The muscles closing the jaw largely fill the side plane of the head

90

Plate 23. MUSCLES OF THE HEAD

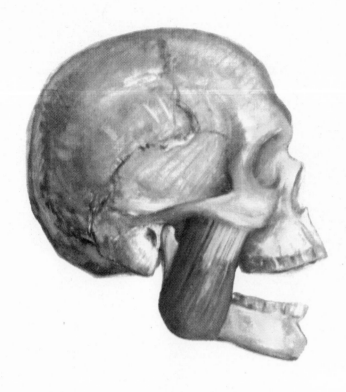

MASSETER
from zygomatic arch
to angle of jaw

TEMPORAL
from temporal ridge
to coronoid process of mandible

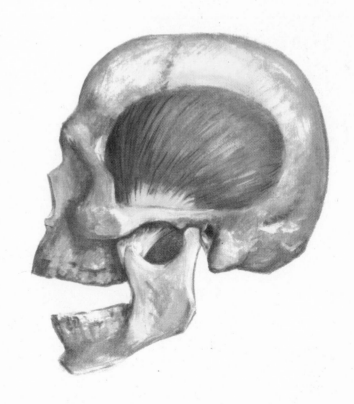

Plate 24. MUSCLES OF THE FACE

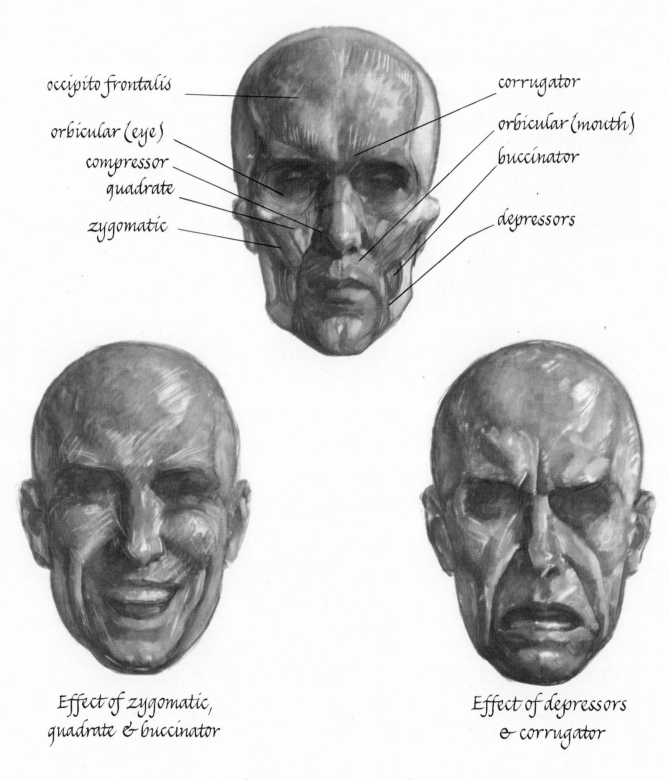

occipito frontalis

orbicular (eye)

compressor

quadrate

zygomatic

corrugator

orbicular (mouth)

buccinator

depressors

Effect of zygomatic,
quadrate & buccinator

Effect of depressors
& corrugator

Zygomatic, quadrate, buccinator & depressors
arise from the bones of the face & are inserted
in the corners of the mouth & in the lips.

ing, the smaller facts of these structures are not indispensable for drawing purposes.[1] In fact, a study of the merely scientific details would actually hinder the student by tending to cultivate the very opposite kind of vision from the one desired. Furthermore, his positive needs are so numerous that there is no room for the superfluous.

In considering the form of the face, it is unnecessary, then, to attempt a minute separation of the many small muscles that are delicately knit together to form one mass comprising cheeks, mouth, and chin. For, if great differentiation is made between these small merging muscles, the inevitable result is the loss of comprehension of the essential form. This *general form* of the face must always be the first consideration, for to the artist this form is more important than the intricate system of muscles that comprise it.

The muscles of the face need to be considered in a big way

The muscles of expression are much softer and more flexible than those of other parts of the body and differ from others in not being inserted in the bone, but in the *skin*.

It is sufficient to regard the muscles of the face as forming roughly two groups: those that draw outward and upward and those that draw downward or inward. One set is expansive; the other, contractive in its effect.

Expansive group. Of the first group, the *zygomatic* and *quadrate* pull from the cheekbones, where they originate. The *buccinator* comes from the maxilla and the mandible. All three are attached to the skin of the corners of the mouth and lips and so, in acting, stretch the lips over the teeth. As they contract, they increase the fullness of the cheeks and exert pressure against the lower lids. In addition, the chin becomes more prominent, for the underlying bone formation is more apparent as the tissues are tightly stretched over it by the action of the muscles of the cheeks. The fundamental effect of the action of this group is due to the stretching of the muscles of mouth, chin, nose, and forehead as they are pulled from the midline *outward and*

The effect of the EXPANSIVE muscles is to pull outward & upward

[1] In Plate 24, the skull is covered in front only by the muscles of the face, the form of the nose being complete for more naturalistic effect. Ears, hair, and muscles of mastication have been omitted, in order to isolate the face muscles. For a similar reason, the hair has not been included in the drawings showing the effect of the contractive and the expansive muscles. As these drawings are designed only to show the *effects* of the two muscular groups, in them the study of expression is merely incidental.

The contractive muscles have the effect of pulling largely downward & inward

upward. This produces an *expanding effect* upon the form of the face, as illustrated.

Contractive group. The second group—*corrugator, compressor,* and *depressors*—as their names imply, draw the masses oppositely to that of the first group, the corrugator contracting the brows and the depressors pulling down the corners of the mouth and the lower lip. The *orbicular* muscles of eye and mouth contract the lids and the lips, respectively. The compressor contracts the nostrils and wrinkles the nose. With this group, the direction of the action is chiefly downward or inward, producing a general *tightening* effect.

All the face muscles are subordinate to the structure of the skull. Their movements govern the delicate variations of facial expression caused by particular emotions experienced by the individual at the moment. As this is fleeting and superficial, we must go underneath to the bones to get at the fundamental form of the head (page 28).

Through half-closed eyes, notice how the head suggests the skull. Drawings of heads should express the bone structure.

The muscles of the face are subordinate to the bone structure

Occipitofrontalis. The thin occipitofrontalis, which runs from the base of the skull and up over it to the line of the brows, fails to conceal the bone structure beneath; and the variations in the form here are caused principally by the skull, except when the muscle is contracted, as in raising the brows.

The subcutaneous cheekbones, nasal bones, and border of the jaw are fixed forms, unaffected in their appearance by any muscular structure.

CONTOUR. Every artist knows that the essence of beauty is far more than "skin deep," to limit the reference strictly to the physical, and that usually, indeed, beauty is largely a matter of *contour*—not so much one of skin texture or particulars of feature, important as these qualities are. In attributing the fine look of a face to some detail of feature, we often lose sight of the larger fact of the contour of the face, which is fundamentally responsible for its beauty. This brings us back to basic things, for contour depends upon bones. A broken bone alters the contour of the part surprisingly.

Contour is fundamental in the structure of the head

Sometimes lovely eyes are set in an ill-shaped face and, for all their loveliness, cannot make it attractive. But we also find features that are not individually fine occurring in a face that is made attractive by its fine contour. It is true, however, that when contour is good it is likely to be uniformly good. The form of forehead, cheek, chin, jaw, nose, mouth, and eyes—in short, the large and the small forms alike—are then found to be interesting in their character.

The attribute of contour is so fundamental in the head that it persists well into maturity and beyond. It is the characteristic by which the individual is first recognized. Contour is the element of permanence in the head. In time, the face may become lined, the muscles may lose some of their resiliency; but as long as the teeth remain, the fundamental form is quite the same for many years. At a little distance, the appearance of the face at fifty is strikingly like the one we knew when the individual was but twenty. This fact is significant, as it indicates the purely superficial character of the small surface details and their comparative unimportance.

Although the quality of contour is perhaps most noticeable on the head, still its influence upon anatomical form is unrestricted. Whether delicate or positive, contour may add its distinctive style to the figure of a child, the back of an athlete, or the hand of a woman.

THE HAIR. The hair should frame the face. The forms of the hair superimpose their own planes over the cranium. These must be organized with reference to the general contour of the skull. They should complement the forms of the face and may often contribute much to the rhythm of the head. It should be borne in mind that, although they are of soft texture, the waves of the hair are nevertheless *definite form* and that they have character, like any solid form. These forms need to be studied and blocked out in their relation to the other forms of the head.

In the blacks of the hair (and even so-called blond hair has surprisingly dark shadows), there is a fine chance for accent, to give contrast with the light skin. But the darker color of hair must never supersede its form.

Contour defines the character of the form & is the element of permanence in the head

In the hair, the emphasis is upon FORM rather than upon color

The hair is subordinate to the skull structure

The line of the hair against the face should be carefully noted. Look for places where the hair blends softly into the flesh. There will be other points where there is a sharp edge as a mass of hair comes crisply against the skin. The observation of these things contributes desirable variety to the drawing.

Hair is usually darker than the skin, but the opposite relation may exist in types where the skin is swarthy and the hair very light; or in a gray-haired Negro type. High lights on glossy hair are high in key, like the high lights on silk or metal. A common mistake, however, is to make them too light.

The hair may suggest the head and face. From the back, for instance, we may form a very definite idea of the face, so suggestive is the hair. That this idea is not always accurate is beside the point. Everyone has had the experience of forming a favorable imaginative idea of someone's appearance from the back, only to be disillusioned when the person turned around. But to compensate us, the reverse may also occur.

The hair has a modifying influence upon the silhouette of the head—on top, at the sides, below, or at some other point.

The highlights on hair need to be controlled

THE FEATURES

As is true of any forms, detailed directions for drawing a feature cannot be given; but we can examine the structural characteristics of features and apply that knowledge in constructing them.

In drawing the features, it is the *larger facts of form*, not the details, that need to be stressed. At first, one is prone to accentuate little things and to draw continuous outlines around every part. Nothing could be worse. It is the big planes of the masses and the way that they fit together which really constitute the structure and which, when constructed, give the true character of the feature. A single feature could hardly be considered without the forms that surround it (Plate 24).

First suggestion of the features

As the details of features are so vast and the types of features so numerous, it is practicable only to point out what to look for. The basic structure is the same in all types. The living model is indispensable where the utmost in character is to be achieved. Draw the block form first. Forms lighted at an angle reveal their planes most strongly.

The essence of the features lies in the BIG FORMS

Of the features, only the ear is stationary. The nose (cartilage portion) has slight movement, the eyes have a considerable range of movement, and the mouth has extreme mobility. In form, the nose is the most obvious; then the ear. The eye is the most accented, and the mouth is the most subtle of the features.

The construction begins with the block form

THE EYE. The construction of the eye begins with the socket. This is the setting for the eyeball. Over the eyeball fit the lids. These, like most anatomical form, need to be drawn with a sweep, to give the feeling of their movement over the eyeball.

97

The setting for the eye comes first

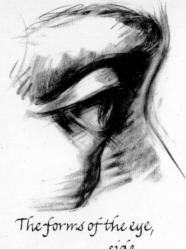

The forms of the eye,
side

The proper relating
of the eyes requires that
they should be
constructed together

Unlike the other features, the eye is often largely in shadow, a fact that contributes to its mystery. It is set in a retreating plane—the plane of the socket. Thus the eye socket becomes the fundamental structure. The brow is set at the upper boundary of the socket, where it meets the plane of the forehead. The outer lines of the lids follow those of the socket.

Although eyes are of many kinds, all have certain things in common. The eyes should be *constructed together*, not separately. They can be made to go together properly by this related study. The opening between the lids is not symmetrical, but is based upon a parallelogram. An eye's width separates the eyes. The upper lid is the heavier and overlaps the under lid at the outer corner, which is slightly higher than the inner corner. The latter is formed by a small bay and is a fixed point in the head, useful in construction. The upper lashes also are the heavier, and their shadow cast on the eyeball lends accent to the lid boundary. Under normal conditions, the only dark accents are at the lower line of the upper lid and the cornea. All the rest is extremely delicate modeling.

The under lid is usually thinner than the upper and, in ordinary lighting, has *no distinct outline* against the eyeball. The mark of the socket is seen where it makes a change of plane with the cheek, below the inner corner of the eye. The socket shows as a triangular depression between the upper lid and the origin of the nose. At the outer side, there is a prominence above the lid that goes back at an angle to the surface of the cheekbone below.

Like the head itself, the eye mass has definite front and side planes of its own. The front and side planes of the lids are small but they conform to the eyeball, just as the lips conform to the teeth. When the eyes look straight out, the lower boundary of the cornea, or colored portion, meets the under lid, but its upper fourth is covered by the upper lid. The white of the eye is not white and must be modeled,

The planes of the eye
exist within the plane of the eye socket

as it is part of the curved surface of the eyeball. The alternation of advancing and retreating planes determines the light and shade, as on a molding. From the side, the front plane slants backward in opposition to the advancing plane of the cheek.

The form of the eye as a whole is best seen when the eye is closed or looking down, for then the plane of the eye socket is intact and the form of the eyeball within it is plainly seen. In this action of the eye, the outer corner appears lower than the inner corner, as the upper lid laps over the under lid.

The brows closely follow the boundary of the sockets. Their effect upon the character of the eye is important and they accent the change of plane from the forehead to the eye sockets.

As in the case of the mouth, the wide range of expressions that characterize the eye is fundamentally caused by the voluntary or involuntary thought of the individual at the moment, giving rise to movements of the expansive or the contractive muscles of the face.

Eyes have to be kept *suggestive*. There are many details involved. These, if rendered meticulously, will inevitably destroy the big form. Much more life results from keeping the eyes simple and suggestive, and the large form is thereby maintained.

THE NOSE. The nose arises from the broad front plane of the face. It is like a modified triangular pyramid with one side set against the face. Below the nasal bones the nose is formed of cartilage, and there is more or less prominence at the bridge, where cartilage and bone join (page 125).

The under triangular plane containing the nostrils connects to the face by curved wings. See the nostrils as part of the under plane of the nose. The sharp movement where the wings of the nostrils swing out from the front plane of the face is of prime importance, as it produces a sharp accent where it curls around into the face. The prominent end portion of the nose occurs in all sorts of forms, which are best studied in profile. The end plane turns abruptly into the under plane by a wedge. The structure here is characteristic, in some degree, of all types.

Construction of the nose, showing under plane

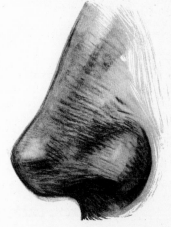

Construction of the nose, profile

It is the basic form that is important

The nose is not
a separate entity, but is
ONE WITH THE FACE.
Outlines should
be suppressed

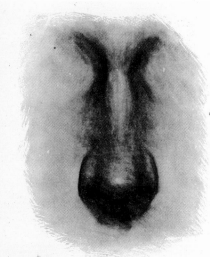

The ear
requires
careful relating
to the head

Through their middle, the side planes of the nose blend with the plane of the face more than they do above and below.

Where light comes against light, there is nothing to define an edge; and no boundary line should be used where the light front plane of the nose comes against the light front plane of the face, as in the three-quarter view. Such an outline gives a false accent, causing detachment of the nose from the face (page 94).

With its varied planes, some part of the nose is foreshortened in any view.

THE EAR. Ears are probably the most slighted of all features. Doubtless this is partly because of their relatively obscure location as the head is seen from the front. Yet ears are fascinating in their rhythmic convolutions and merit careful study. Like other features, ears vary in size and type, but they usually fall within the lines of the brow and the base of the nose. Much of the effect of the ear from the front depends upon this proper relationship, which will vary considerably with the action of the head (pages 125 and 126).

As the ear opening falls just back of the middle of the skull, the entire ear is back of this line. A common fault is to place the ear too far forward. From the side, the ear needs to be carefully related in position and direction to the jaw, the zygomatic arch, and the back of the head. In three-quarter back view, the ear often exhibits a double curve.

The ear is naturally divided into three parts: rim, bowl, and lobe. Its long axis parallels the nose. Outside the bowl is a secondary rim. From the side, we look into the bowl; and from the back, we see the outside of it. The rim and the lobe are more detached from the head. There are two main planes, one running downward and backward within the rim, and the other running across the lobe. Reject

Forms of the ear
from back

Reject small details
& keep
the ear simple

details, but coordinate the planes in the ear. The ear needs to be kept simple. It should be seen and *rendered as a whole*, rather than part by part. *Avoid doing too much to an ear.*

THE MOUTH. The lower zone of the face includes, of course, the mouth and the chin.

As with the eye, so with the mouth, the underlying bone structure is the basis of the form. The teeth are set on the form of a half cylinder and the covering of muscle follows that form, giving the lips and the chin definite front and side planes. The front plane is roughly determined by prolonging the diverging lines of the septum of the upper lip.

The modeling surrounding the mouth is of first importance in establishing the character of the lower part of the face. And this portion of the face is the most subtle, because of the delicate form and the great mobility of the muscles of the region. The mouth conforms to the semicylindrical maxilla and mandible, with their teeth. The plane above the lips belongs to the general front plane of the face, whose boundaries diverge to the cheekbones. Outside the corners of the mouth are full forms, carrying down toward the jaw. At the sides, the fullness of the mouth above creates some subtle modeling, which greatly affects the expression. A strong depression occurs under the lower lip, above the chin projection.

The septum is a delicately modeled form and, in ordinary lighting, should be merely suggested. Accenting its lines gives it undue importance and tends to destroy the simple modeling of the mouth.

Lips are merely a part of the mouth and often, a minor part, for full lips belong only to certain types. The red portions of the lips are delicate in their forms. As in the case of the eyes, the *lips should be taken together*. They form one mass. The lips project and there are soft depressions where they turn in at the corners.

Aside from the stronger pigmentation of the lips themselves, the thing that accentuates them is their planes. This is especially true of the full-lipped type. The lower lip is given form by the depression under its middle portion. This depression reaches to the advancing

The forms
AROUND THE MOUTH
constitute the basic structure of the region

The lips form ONE MASS

Thin-lipped type

The lips have distinct planes of their own

Modeling of the mouth,
three-quarter

Modeling of the mouth,
profile

Construction of the mouth
from the side

Modeling of the mouth,
lips parted

plane of the chin. In the same way, the upper lip owes its character to the way its plane opposes both the plane above and the plane of the lower lip below.

The plane of the upper lip is flatter and more angular than that of the lower, which is softly rounded, with a slight depression in the center. Into this fits the little prominence in the center of the upper lip. The boundary of the red portion against the surface above often takes a line surprisingly like an archery bow.

The lower lip is usually heavier and somewhat more full than the upper. Though at the middle it separates markedly from the plane beneath it, on the sides the lip forms part of the general plane of the chin. Therefore, *this red portion should not be outlined*. It represents a change of color, not of form.

The three full forms that fit together at the middle are useful in gaining a conception of the mouth. From the side, the great variety in direction found in the lines of the mouth and chin interestingly suggests the mobility of the feature. As with the eye and the nose, this series of advancing and retreating planes is very significant as a determinant of form. But there are many mouths in which the lips are merely suggested. Notice the lips in a group of people.

In the mouth with lips parted, as in smiling, the teeth become important. The lips not only are stretched upward but backward over the teeth, and so lose much of their normal shape. Significant are the accents at the corners, the shadow under the upper lip, and the upper row of teeth. The folds or dimples on each side of the mouth and the stretching of the skin over the chin are other conditions accompanying the smile.

The chin is a wedge jutting out from the wings flanking the mouth on each side. Only the *forms around the mouth* can tie the mouth to the face.

As in all form, one needs to keep constantly to the *general effect*. Complete no single part of the drawing until *all* parts are organized and related. A common fault is to overaccent subtleties of form, such as the boundaries of the septum of the nose, the delicate fold from wing of nostril to corner of mouth, the nostrils, the line of the lower

Use simple, broad treatment, disregarding details

lid, and the line of the lower lip. Such misplaced attention to details results in exaggeration and destroys the unity of the head. There is one unbroken plane from cheekbone to upper lip, and the pyramidal-shaped nose is set upon this plane.

Study the head through half-closed eyes, use a mirror or a reducing glass, and frequently go back to view the model and your drawing from across the room. These expedients give breadth and freshness of vision and help the draughtsman to get strength into his work.

Practical aids in study

THE CHARCOAL TECHNIQUE. For life drawing, the charcoal medium is unexcelled. It can be handled in the greatest variety of techniques and works with the utmost facility. Moreover, it is easily erased or worked over. According to its use, charcoal can be both a delicate and a forceful medium. It is most sensitive in its response. No restriction should be placed upon its use—the more freely it is used, the better.

Charcoal is the most facile of mediums

The construction is done with the medium-hard variety of charcoal brought to a long, fine point by wearing down on the sand pad (pages 18, 72, 81, and 133). Then the modeling of the forms in their values and light and shade is developed by line and tone. Here the softer charcoal may be introduced for the darks (pages 94, 118, and 180).

Line, with tone modeled by the fingers, produces good technique

A combination of line and of tones modeled with the fingers yields the best results. Tones are built up with fine charcoal lines and the lights are modeled out of the tone by white lines made with a small bit of kneaded rubber (misnamed "eraser"), brought to an edge. Of course, it is necessary to pinch the rubber to a new edge as fast as it flattens out under pressure (pages 129 and 153).

The kneaded rubber adds variety by means of white line

In this building up of the forms by line and tone, the interesting texture of the charcoal-paper grain provides a varied and unifying quality to the drawing and should be exploited (pages 97 and 123).

Another effective method of using charcoal is to cover a portion of the paper with a thick tone of charcoal, smoothed over somewhat with the chamois skin. The drawing in line is then made over this tone, after which the modeling is done by wiping out the lights—

Working out of a tone emphasizes modeling

using the chamois, the fingers, and the kneaded rubber. Accents of dark are added. Either pencil or charcoal paper is suitable for this technique (pages 28 and 102).

THE PRINCIPLE OF MODELING. Unless lighted from an angle, the form appears as flat pattern.

With light from the back, there is simply silhouette; with the light from in front, all is light and there is only very subtle suggestion of solidity. In both cases the effect is essentially one of flat pattern.

The flat pattern, like the outline-type drawing, often can be made with little thought of the planes; but when the light is from the side, above, or below—*i.e.*, at any angle to the form—the solidity of the form is expressed and then the *masses with their planes* determine the construction.

The form is definitely expressed only when there is strong lighting to give contrast between the planes on one side and those on the other.

To express modeled form, it is necessary to avoid placing the high light along an *edge*.

The principle of modeling is that the highest light occurs somewhere *within the edges* of the form, the tone becoming darker each way toward the boundaries. It is only in the extreme position, where the form is practically silhouetted against the light, that the high light will appear on the edge of the form. But here the form has already been modeled substantially and is not adversely affected by the edge accent.

This can be readily demonstrated with an ovoid representing, in a simple way, the head or other anatomical part.

Lighting greatly affects the appearance of the form

The principle of modeling. In simple lighting, the high light is WITHIN THE FORM

Position C

Position B

MODEL

Position A

Direction of Light

PRINCIPLE OF MODELING

Effect from A: Light & halftones only, no shadow

Effect from B: Light halftone & shadow but high light INSIDE THE EDGE

Effect from C: Only from unusual angle such as this would high light occur on the edge

EDGES. Outline is a convenient convention for limiting a form in space, and the linear accent in a tone study may contribute great variety. Forms in nature, of course, are not outlined and do not commonly suggest line, but the eye is stimulated by the ever-changing variety of the edges of forms. There is constant alternation as a sharply defined edge cuts crisply against its contrasting background, then loses itself against a ground of its own tone (page 118).

At one point, the form will be light against dark and, at another, dark against light. But when the tone of the form and that of the background are similar, there is no definition and one tone blends with the other.

This occurs frequently in tone study and can be anticipated in color interpretation, as well, though here there are complications; for a form which in value is identical with its ground may still be defined by its contrasting color.

PORTRAITURE. In portraiture, it is especially necessary to be able to do a perfect job of construction. There is only one head in the world like that of the subject, and if you are doing a portrait of that one, you will have to particularize in the highest degree. It would be embarrassing to paint a person and then have it appear more like someone else or, worse still, like no one! A portrait is a character study and should emphasize the character of the subject. Inevitably, but *only incidentally, will it express the personality of the artist.*

To achieve the character of the form in a head is primarily a matter of construction: first, the composition, then the proportions and relations of all the parts of the head one to another, then the modeling of the forms. It is a common fault for the student to become preoccupied with the eye or the lips and to slight the larger forms. The setting of the eyes is of larger importance than the eyes themselves, and it must logically be given first attention. The setting for the eyes includes the forehead, eye sockets, cheekbones, and nasal bones.

The forms surrounding the mouth, though subtle, are of the utmost importance, for they determine the expression of the face. The term *expression* is here used in its broader sense. Not mere sign of

Seek VARIETY in your treatment of the boundaries of forms

Portraiture demands exact construction

Work in general terms, perfecting the larger forms first

emotion but that positive form relation encompassing mouth, chin, jaw, teeth, and upper and lower lips is what is meant.

There is, however, a moment when all things are finally coordinated and a vital portrait of the subject is achieved. Just how this occurs the artist does not know; for he does not project his personality into the work consciously. It is simultaneous.

The result is the culmination of the search for form relationships, the careful modeling, the adjustment of color, and the sympathetic handling, which finally matures into a composed unit. This is a record of the individual as the artist conceives him. A good portrait transcends the material properties of which it is made and radiates only a personality.

Complete organization is imperative

The smaller forms are considered last

THE TRUNK II

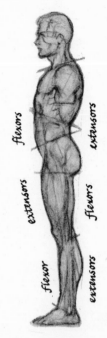

MUSCLES MOVING THE TRUNK. Muscles connecting the main parts of the figure oppose one another from front to back and from above downward.

Long muscles running between the pelvis and the rib cage bend the body forward or straighten and strain it backward.

Erector spinae. In the back is a powerful column, which starts on the sacrum and back quarter of the iliac crest and rises along both sides of the spinal column up to the base of the skull. It fills in the space between the angles of the ribs, and its fibers are attached to the ribs as well as to the dorsal vertebrae. Though actually it is composed

Muscles having opposite functions are alternated on the figure

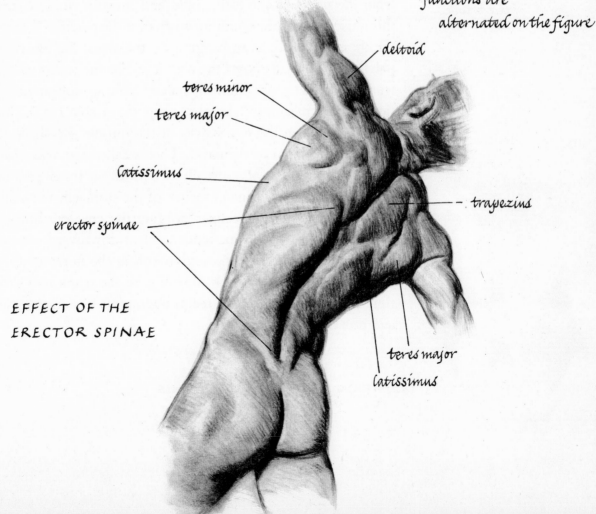

deltoid

teres minor

teres major

latissimus

trapezius

erector spinae

EFFECT OF THE
ERECTOR SPINAE

teres major

latissimus

of several separate muscles, for our purpose it may reasonably be regarded as one mass.

As the spinal column is the only bony part between the rib cage and the pelvis, powerful muscles are required to sustain the body. The cross section through the lumbar region gives an idea of the bulk of these two masses bulging one each side of the column. They act to extend the vertebral column, thus bringing the trunk from the bent forward position to the erect position. They also bend the column backward.

This muscular mass is called the *erector spinae*, because of its location and because it holds the trunk erect. It is entirely covered by other muscles, except a small portion (the splenius) that crops out in the neck region. But its influence upon the lower part of the back is considerable, as the spinae here forms the main mass, the portions of muscles that overlay it in this part being thin in character. The construction suggests a *wedging* into the hip mass (pages 114, 132, and Plate 1).

Rectus abdominis. On the front of the trunk is the rectus abdominis, a band of muscle forming the middle plane and reaching from the pubis to the fifth, sixth, and seventh ribs. In contracting, this muscle bends the trunk forward; or if the position is one in which the thorax is fixed, as in hanging by the arms, the muscle pulls the pelvis up. Plate 26 shows the abdominis in the action of flexing the trunk. The rectus abdominis is named from its appearance and location—*rectus* meaning "straight" (pages 113 and 122). The vertical division between the two halves of the muscle is a shallow groove, well marked down to the navel. This is called the *linea alba* ("white line"). The muscle also usually shows three transverse lines: one just above the navel, one at the pit of the stomach, and a third about midway between. These lines provide the characteristic pattern of the region. The upper line tends to slant downward somewhat as it runs outward, and the others approximate the horizontal.

While lying on the back, slowly raise the trunk to a sitting position. In this movement, the rectus abdominis is working and its bulk and power may be felt.

The rectus abdominis provides a characteristic design on the front of the trunk

ISOLATION OF RECTUS ABDOMINIS

Plate 25. EXTENSOR OF THE TRUNK

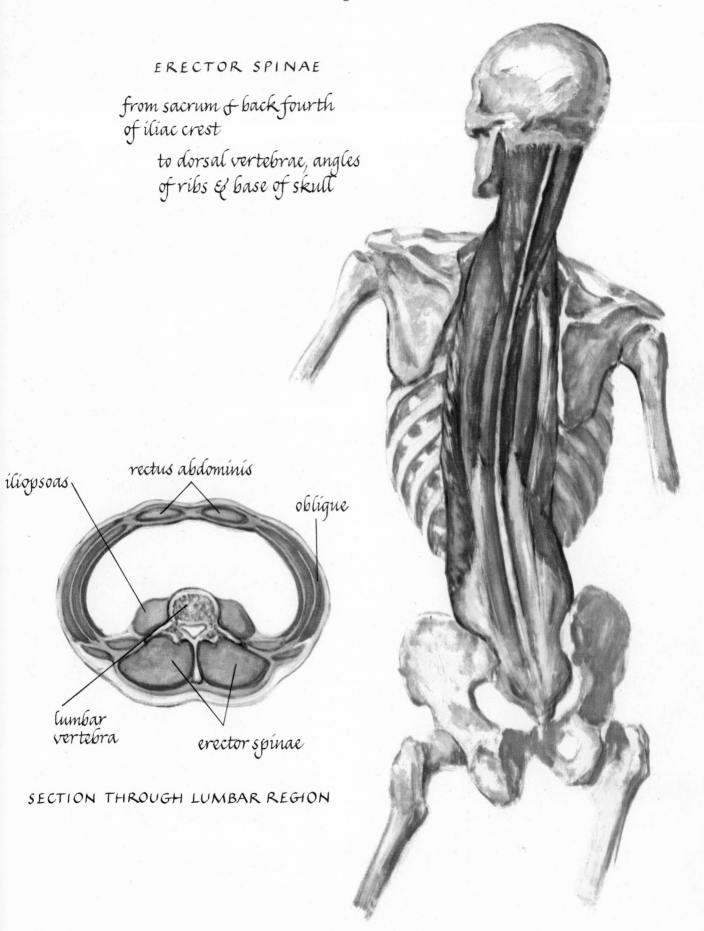

ERECTOR SPINAE

from sacrum & back fourth
of iliac crest

to dorsal vertebrae, angles
of ribs & base of skull

iliopsoas

rectus abdominis

oblique

lumbar
vertebra

erector spinae

SECTION THROUGH LUMBAR REGION

Plate 26. FLEXORS OF THE TRUNK

RECTUS ABDOMINIS
from pubis
    to 5th, 6th & 7th ribs

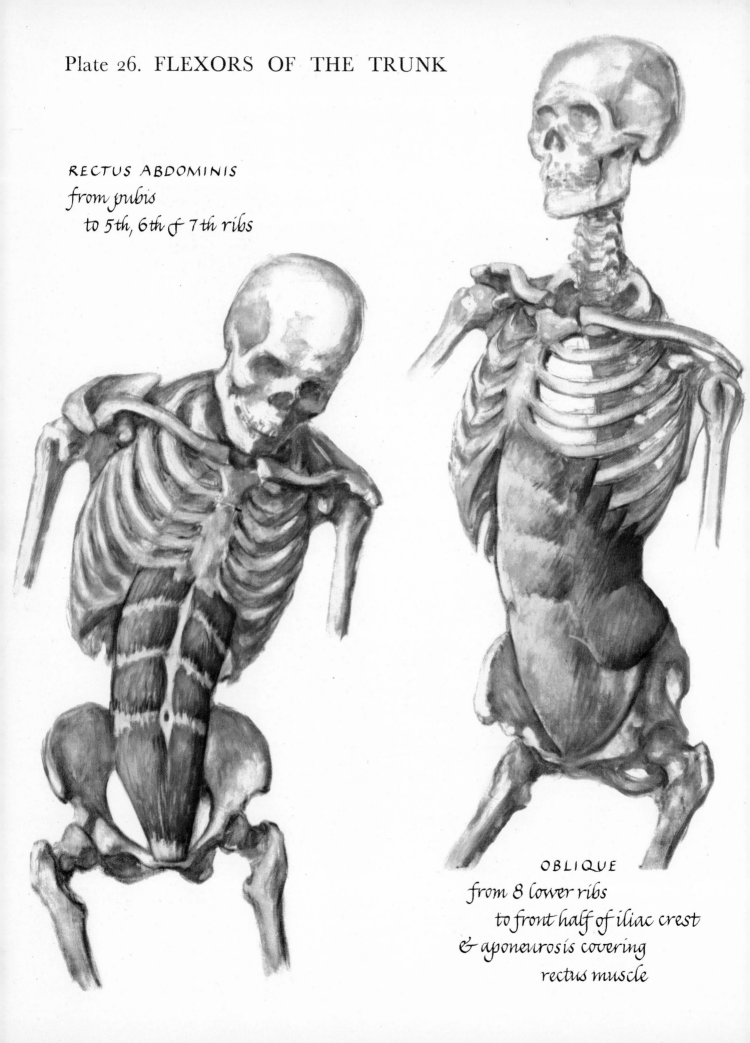

OBLIQUE
from 8 lower ribs
    to front half of iliac crest
& aponeurosis covering
        rectus muscle

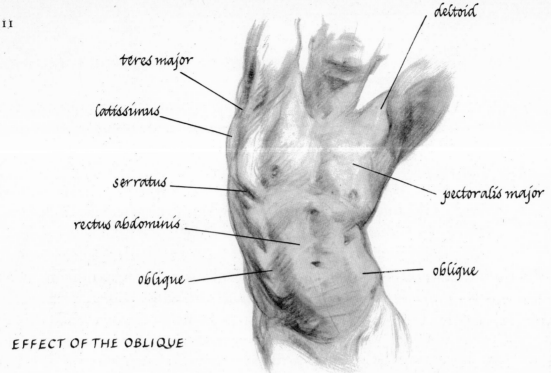

teres major

deltoid

latissimus

serratus

pectoralis major

rectus abdominis

oblique

oblique

EFFECT OF THE OBLIQUE

Oblique. Closely related to the abdominis and bordering it on the side, is the oblique. As the name implies, this mass runs obliquely, by digitations from the eight lower ribs to the front half of the iliac crest. A well-defined groove marks its connection with the rectus abdominis. From this line the oblique sends an aponeurosis, or thin tendinous sheet, out over the rectus abdominis, reinforcing it. The muscle terminates below in *Poupart's ligament*, a tough band stretching between the upper iliac spine and the pubis and giving the characteristic semicircular form to the lower boundary of the abdomen— a line that is fundamental in blocking in the figure.

From the cross-section diagram, it will be observed that the oblique is only one of three layers of muscles overlapping to form the wall of the flank. The three together furnish the bulk that we impute to the oblique as the superficial muscle of the group. Between the crest and the ribs is the thick portion of the mass. As shown in the illustration, the oblique brings the pelvis toward the thorax, or vice versa. Therefore, whenever the body weight is shifted, the oblique on the side bearing the weight pulls the thorax over toward that

Poupart's ligament
marks the
lower boundary of the trunk

side. The oblique of the opposite, or inactive, side is then extended (page 179).

Together, the rectus abdominis and the oblique comprise the whole mass of the lower two-thirds of the trunk as seen from the front (pages 113 and 122).

MUSCLES MOVING THE ARM. The other muscles of the trunk have as their primary function the moving of the arm.

Certain of these muscles arise from the trunk and act upon the arm indirectly through their attachment to the shoulder girdle.

Others move the arm directly, some running from the shoulder girdle to the humerus and others from the trunk to the humerus.

Some of the muscles that originate on the trunk and are inserted in the shoulder girdle are covered, or largely covered, by surface muscles; but they are fundamental as forces moving the scapula and, with it, the arm. In their effect upon the figure, they count with the muscles that cover them.

Rhomboids. The rhomboids have their origin along the spinal column, extending in a line from about the fourth cervical to the fifth dorsal vertebra. They run obliquely downward and outward (beneath the trapezius) to the inner border of the scapula. A small triangle of the rhomboid at the lower part of its attachment sometimes shows on the surface, between the muscles overlapping it. The rhomboids assist in the rotation of the scapula.

Levator. Grouped with the rhomboids is the levator ("raiser") of the scapula. It springs from the lateral spines of the first four cervical vertebrae and swings down to its insertion in the upper angle of the scapula. Thus its attachments are just above those of the rhomboids. A portion of the levator appears on the side of the neck, in front of the trapezius. The levator acts in raising the scapula at its upper angle.

Pectoralis minor. The trunk origin of the pectoralis minor occurs (under the pectoralis major) on the third, fourth, and fifth ribs. But the muscle sometimes evidences itself when it acts in depressing the scapula at the coracoid process, where it is attached.

Many muscles located on the trunk move the shoulder & the arm

The rhomboids, levator, & pectoralis minor are largely hidden, but they have mechanical importance

To summarize, in the action of rotating the scapula, the rhomboids pull upward from the lower inner corner of their insertion, while the pectoralis minor cooperates in the action by pulling downward from the upper, outer side of the blade.

Serratus. The serratus, named from the saw-toothed character of the line of its origin, sends fibers from each of the eight upper ribs to the inner border of the scapula. The points of its origin describe an arc on the ribs. The origin of the serratus coincides in part with that of the oblique, the two muscles having the *middle four ribs as origin in common.* The serratus fits *between the rib cage and the scapula,* so that a large part of it is covered by the bladebone.[1] As has been stated, it is attached along the inner border of the scapula.

[1] The structure of the serratus is explained in the schematic drawing. The scapula has been pulled away to reveal the portion of the serratus lying underneath. Only the shaded portion is superficial. Muscles of the chest and back cover the rest of the muscle, as shown by the boundary lines.

The rhomboids & the pectoralis minor act together in rotating the scapula

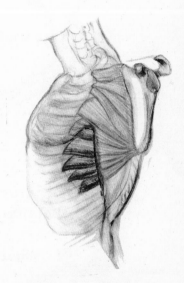

Superficial portion of serratus, shaded

Dotted line indicates boundary of muscles which overlap serratus

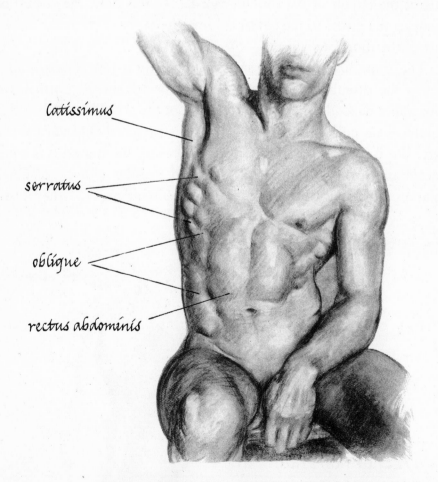

latissimus

serratus

oblique

rectus abdominis

EFFECT OF SERRATUS FROM FRONT

The serratus makes a characteristic pattern on the side of the trunk

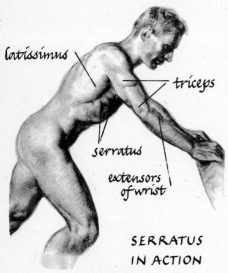

latissimus

triceps

serratus

extensors of wrist

SERRATUS
IN ACTION

Though only a small part of the serratus is in evidence on the model, the muscle is important, as it forms one of the most characteristic features of the side of the trunk (page 122). It appears prominently, as it acts to rotate or pull the scapula forward in such actions of the arm as occur when pushing or lunging forward. The serratus is, therefore, often called the *fencer's muscle*. The typical action is illustrated on the opposite page.

Trapezius. One of the most interesting of muscles, from the standpoint of design, is the trapezius ("table" muscle), which really resembles a winged creature or an airplane in its pattern. Its streamlined styling suggests movement.

The trapezius occupies the upper part of the back, neck, and shoulders. Starting from the base of the skull, the cervical and the 12 dorsal vertebrae, it spreads out over the back, its fibers converging to the spine of the scapula, the acromion, and on around, over the outer third of the clavicle. Its insertion thus coincides with a large part of the circuit of the shoulder girdle. In this way, the trapezius connects the girdle to the spinal column, from the skull to the lower part of the thorax (Plate 1).

The trapezius is entirely superficial and it covers almost completely the rhomboids and the levator. Apart from the normal, its appearance depends upon the movement of the shoulders. When the shoulders are pulled forward, the muscle is stretched out over the rib cage. But if the shoulders are drawn backward, the trapezius is contracted and forms two tight rolls, pressed together along the spinal column. In the movement of raising the shoulders, it is the upper

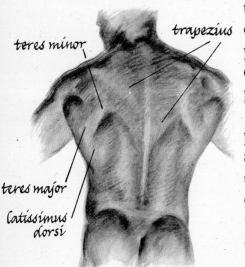

teres minor

trapezius

teres major

latissimus dorsi

EFFECT OF TRAPEZIUS, ARMS OUT

The trapezius, keystone of the back, has many phases

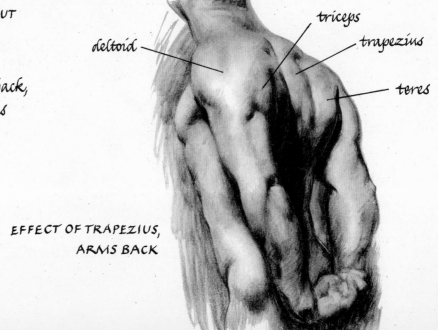

deltoid

triceps

trapezius

teres

EFFECT OF TRAPEZIUS,
ARMS BACK

Plate 27. MUSCLES MOVING THE SHOULDER GIRDLE

LEVATOR OF SCAPULA
from lateral spines, 1st four cervical vertebrae
to upper angle of scapula

PECTORALIS MINOR
from 3rd, 4th & 5th ribs
to coracoid process
of scapula

RHOMBOIDS
from vertebrae, 4th cervical –
5th dorsal
to inner border of scapula

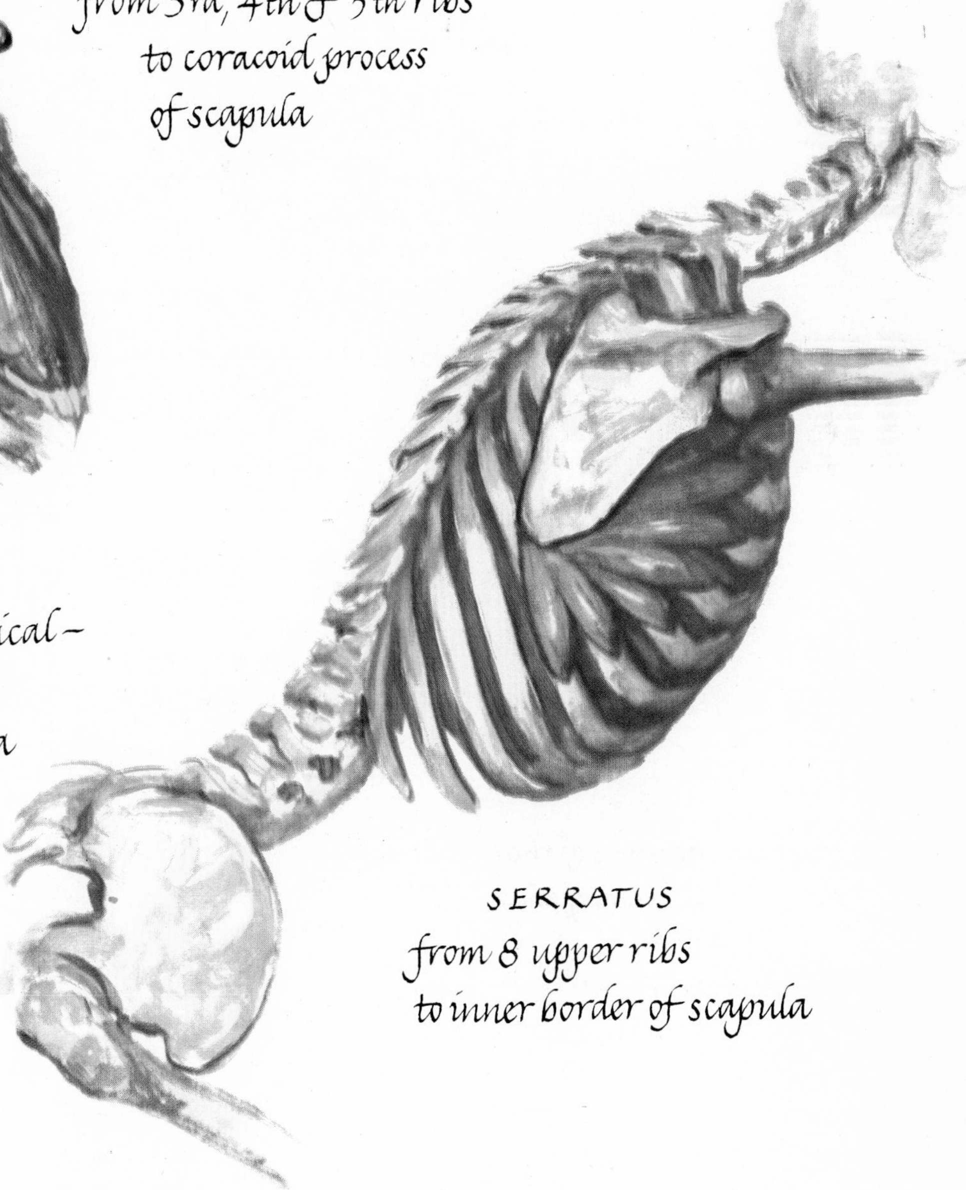

SERRATUS
from 8 upper ribs
to inner border of scapula

Plate 28. MUSCLES MOVING THE SHOULDER GIRDLE

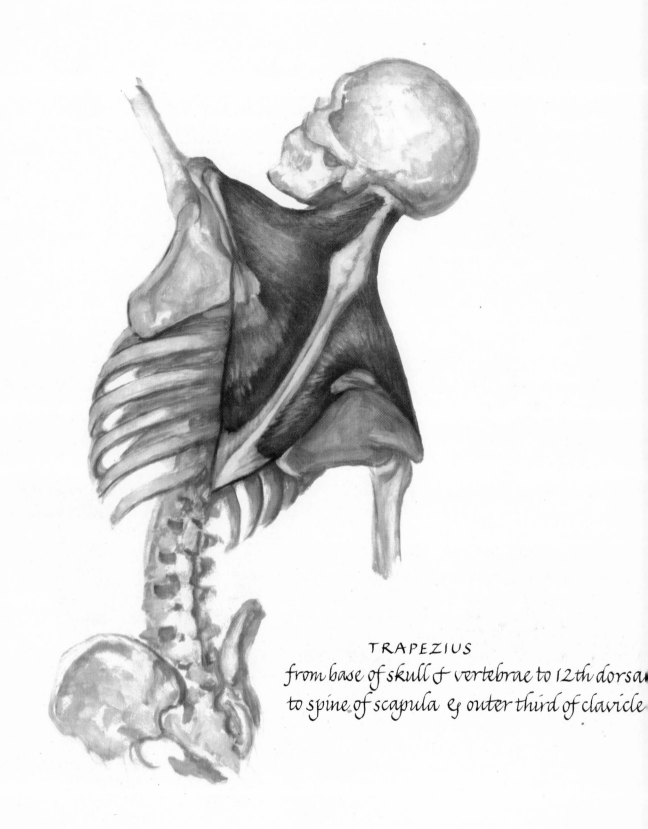

TRAPEZIUS
from base of skull & vertebrae to 12th dorsa
to spine of scapula & outer third of clavicle

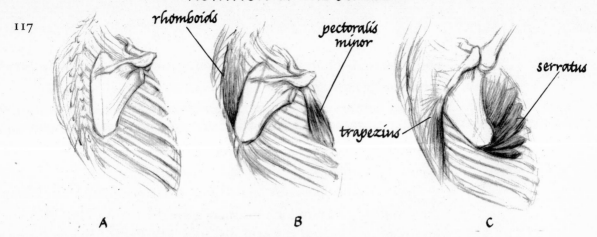

rhomboids

pectoralis minor

serratus

trapezius

A   B   C

A   shows the normal position of the scapula.

In B   the right scapula is rotated clockwise by the rhomboids & pectoralis minor.

In C   the trapezius & serratus act together to rotate the scapula counterclockwise.

portion of the muscle that is acting. Both sides of the trapezius operate in drawing the shoulders back (page 46).

As the arm is raised, various phases of stretching and contraction ensue. The section of the trapezius that extends from the twelfth dorsal vertebra to the inner end of the spine of the scapula acts, with the lower part of the serratus, in rotating the scapula, thus helping to raise the arm (page 118 and 121). This movement is the opposite of that created by the rhomboids and pectoralis minor.

The trapezius & the serratus work in raising the arm

The tendons by which the trapezius is attached to the bones are guideposts for construction on the back. From the skull, short tendons mark out a path down the spine. In this, there is a diamond-shaped area surrounding the prominent seventh cervical vertebra. A similar shape occurs at the twelfth dorsal and still others where the muscle attaches to the inner end of the spine of the scapula. The significance of these spaces is that, being tendon, they remain unchanged when the various parts of the muscle are contracted, and so exist as depressed areas in the surrounding mound of muscle (page 107).

Tendons of the trapezius furnish markings on the back

The trapezius largely forms the neck and the line of the shoulders at the back. It is important also from the front of the figure, forming the line of the shoulder from the neck to the cap of the shoulder. Its boundary continues from here along the outer third of the clavicle

trapezius

TRAPEZIUS FROM FRONT

and, thence, back to the starting point. From the front it appears as a triangular mass each side of the neck.

The borders of the trapezius, between the spines of the scapula and the twelfth dorsal vertebra, may show delicately, though when contracted, this part of the muscle is most prominent just where it leaves the scapula.

Infraspinatus and teres minor. Three sets of muscles originate on the shoulder girdle but are inserted in the humerus. Thus they come into play in working the arm directly. The first of these, the infraspinatus ("under the spine"—of the scapula) and the teres minor (*teres* meaning "round") form one mass, which covers the greater part of the back of the scapula below its spine. The mass passes to its insertion on the back of the tuberosity of the humerus. Its function is to draw the arm backward and to rotate it outward. Though it is largely covered by the deltoid, a bulging triangular area marks its location on the inner side of the scapula (page 114).

Teres major. Associated with the teres minor is the teres major, which at first appears to be a part of the mass above, as it also originates on the scapula, but at its lower angle. However, the teres major has a different insertion. Instead of going out to the back of the tuberosity of the humerus with the teres minor, the teres major cuts through to the front of the humerus and is there inserted in the bicipital groove, inner lip (Plate 42). Its action is to draw down the arm and to rotate it inward. In this latter action it works in opposition to the teres minor.

When acting, the teres major bulges in a full, rounded mass at the base of the scapula. It is more prominent than the teres minor, being one of the more conspicuous forms on the back (page 121). Rotation of the humerus outward and inward brings into play, alternately, the two teres muscles. In Plate 29 the humerus is drawn backward and downward by the action of this group.

Deltoid. The last of the group of muscles having origin on the girdle and insertion in the arm is the deltoid, the muscle that forms the pad of the shoulder. As shown, the deltoid has an extensive origin, arising from the whole length of the spine of the scapula, the acro-

The teres minor appears as one of the triangular forms on the back

The teres major & minor oppose each other in rotating the arm

DELTOID IN ACTION

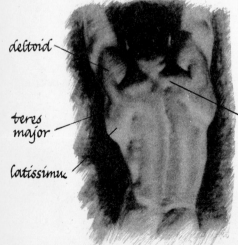

deltoid

teres major

latissimus

trapezius

Plate 29. MUSCLES MOVING THE ARM

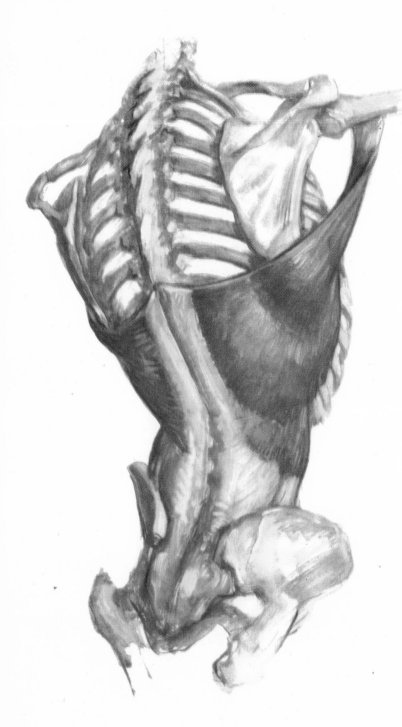

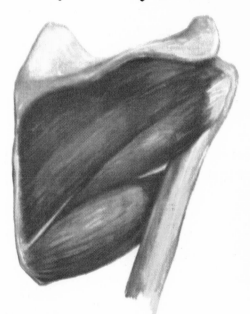

INFRASPINATUS & TERES MINOR
from scapula, below its spine
to back of tuberosity of humerus

TERES MAJOR
from lower angle of scapula
to bicipital groove

LATISSIMUS DORSI
from 7th dorsal, lumbar vertebrae, sacrum,
back third of iliac crest & lower 3 or 4 ribs
to bicipital groove

Plate 30. MUSCLES MOVING THE ARM

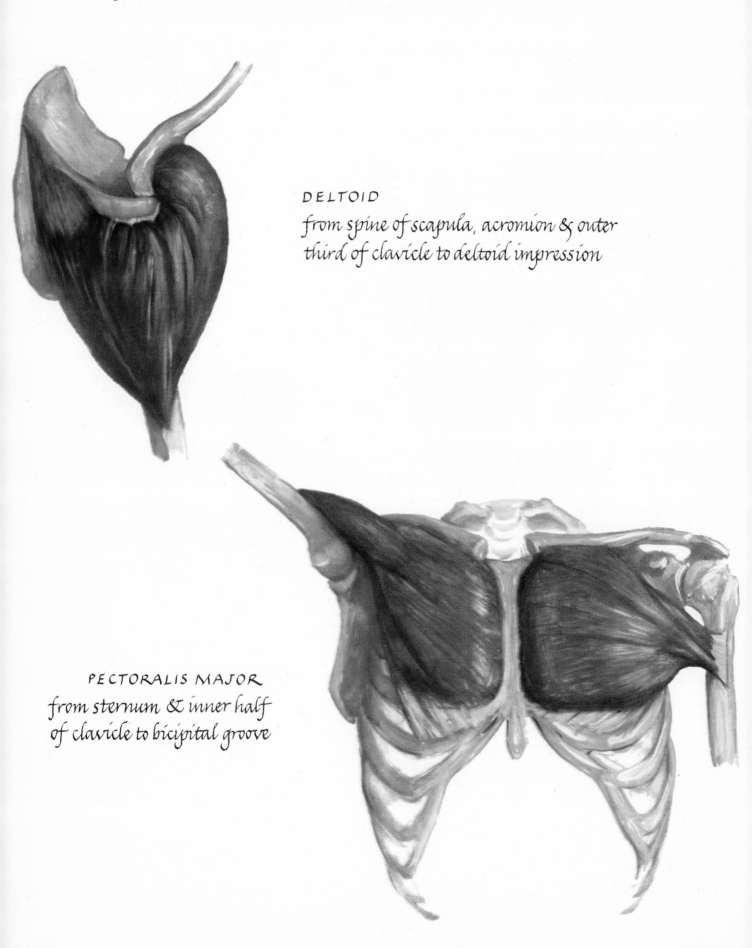

DELTOID
from spine of scapula, acromion & outer
third of clavicle to deltoid impression

PECTORALIS MAJOR
from sternum & inner half
of clavicle to bicipital groove

mion process, and on the front of the shoulders from the outer third of the clavicle. Thus its origin exactly coincides with the insertion of the trapezius.

The viewpoint used in Plate 30 is from above, to give a clear idea of the way in which the deltoid circuits the shoulder. The deltoid has three rather distinct parts, from its three points of origin. The fibers of all converge sharply to the insertion nearly halfway down the humerus in the deltoid impression. With this leverage, the powerful muscle raises the arm. The deltoid is, in fact, commonly known as the great abductor of the arm. Its shape is a very important one in determining the contour of the shoulder. The deltoid is entirely superficial and makes the important bulge of the shoulder in every view (pages 114, 121, 122, 163, 164, 179, and 180).

Two large and extensive muscles constitute the group that originate on the trunk and attach to the humerus. These are the latissimus dorsi ("broadest muscle of the back") and the pectoralis major ("principal chest muscle"). Though the latissimus covers a large area of the back and the pectoralis covers the chest, each is concentrated in a narrow flat band for insertion in the bicipital groove of the humerus, alongside the insertion of the teres major.

Latissimus dorsi. The latissimus dorsi has an extensive origin. On the spinal column, it extends down the lower six dorsal vertebrae, the lumbar vertebrae, the sacrum, on the back third of the iliac crest, and on the lower three or four ribs. Its rib digitations fit with the three or four lower digitations of the oblique. At the iliac crest, a slight hollow marks the space between the latissimus and the oblique (page 107). The latissimus is not thick in its lower portion, but here covers the bulky erector spinae, which counts with it. As it passes from the origin at the lower ribs, the muscle increases in bulk and, when acting, it may be seen as a long, thick mass at the side of the trunk (page 114).

With the arm raised from the side, the latissimus forms the boundary of the back wall of the armpit and, from the front, clearly shows beyond the rib cage. The latissimus has great leverage for operating the arm, as it pulls not only from the thorax but all the way from the

The origin of the deltoid coincides with the insertion of the trapezius

The latissimus dorsi & the pectoralis major connect the trunk to the arm directly

When acting, the latissimus is prominent on the side of the lower rib cage

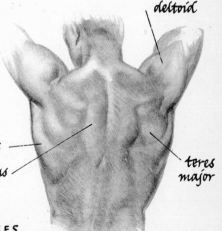

deltoid

latissimus

trapezius

teres major

EFFECT OF LATISSIMUS & TERES

sacrum and the iliac crest. The muscle draws the raised arm downward and backward. This action of the latissimus is illustrated in Plate 29, and the manner of its insertion is shown. Like the teres major, it acts as an internal rotator of the arm and also works in pulling up the trunk by the arms.

The latissimus is superficial, except at its insertion in the front of the humerus. The bandlike terminal portion twists as it approaches its insertion and forms a convenient sling for the teres major.

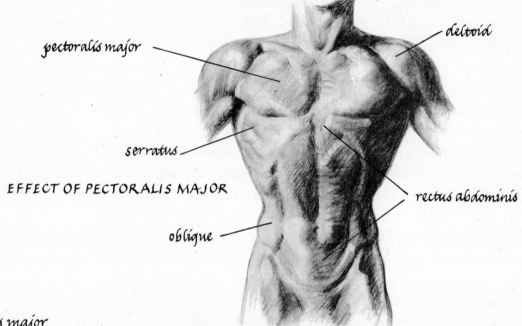

pectoralis major

deltoid

serratus

rectus abdominis

EFFECT OF PECTORALIS MAJOR

oblique

The pectoralis major gives the squared construction to the chest

Pectoralis major. The pectoralis major is shown (Plate 30) in its normal condition, as well as when the arm is raised. The effect of its attachment in the bicipital groove is shown. The muscle twists and reverses as it leaves its origins to attach to the arm, its fibers blending with those of the deltoid. It forms the front wall of the armpit. But when the arm is raised above the head, this wall disappears, as the fibers going to the attachment are untwisted by the elevation of the arm and now pass directly to the bicipital groove, outer lip (pages 111 and 113).

The pectoralis major is of general rectangular shape and produces the squared construction of the chest (page 117). The muscle arises

pectoralis major

from the sternum and the inner half of the clavicle. It is, thus, partly related to the group having their origins on the shoulder girdle. When the muscle is in action, the divisions between the sternal and the clavicular origins are well marked. The pectoralis pulls the arm in toward the body, as may be demonstrated by pressing the hands together in front (page 108). It draws the arm down and also forward, thus opposing the action of the latissimus, which draws it backward. Another powerful action of the pectoralis is to pull up the trunk, as in chinning oneself. The pectoralis is superficial.

In the female, the form of the pectoral muscles is, of course, greatly modified by the breasts. Their full, rounded forms cover the lower and part of the outer boundary of the muscle.

Therefore, movements of the arms that cause a stretching or a compression of the pectoralis naturally alter the form and location of the breasts. Similarly, the pendular nature of the breasts makes gravity a determining factor in their changing appearance.

SUMMARY. Because of its loose attachment to the thorax, the shoulder girdle moves with great freedom. Movements of the arms and shoulders strongly modify the character of the upper half of the trunk, from any view.

When the shoulders are drawn forward, the broad muscles of the back are stretched so tightly over the surface that they lose much of their individual character and expose the form of the cage. The teres muscles, however, are prominent, as they rotate the arm.

With shoulders drawn backward, the arms are brought much closer together and the trapezius and the teres are tightly compressed, so that they appear as firm rolls.

Like the face, the back has "expressions." There is the tight, contracted expression of a frowning face when the shoulders are forced backward; but if the shoulders are brought forward, the open, expansive look of a relaxed countenance is produced.

Raising the arms above the head brings the deltoid into prominence, and the scapulae are swung outward, emphasizing the full

**PECTORALIS REGION
IN THE FEMALE**

*Effect of movement
on breast forms*

*In contraction, the
back muscles superimpose
their bulging forms
        over the frame*

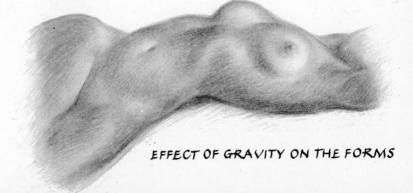

EFFECT OF GRAVITY ON THE FORMS

*In raising the arms,
the deltoid & the upper
trapezius act powerfully*

forms of the teres. The upper part of the trapezius is compressed into two horizontal masses.

Similarly, from the front, with arms brought in close to the body, the pectorals are flexed into two ball forms, which appear very different from the squares of the normal position. The arms, encroaching upon the trunk, greatly narrow its front plane.

From the front, the structure of the armpit is revealed when the arm is raised from the side but, if it is raised above the head, the pit disappears (page 111). Then the merging pectoralis and deltoid cut prominently across the shoulders, concealing the clavicles and the trapezius. In their lower portion, the pectorals are stretched upward over the cage. The latissimus and the teres major are emphasized, as their mass forms the outer boundary of the trunk, cutting across the serratus.

*Raising the arms
stretches the chest
muscles & displaces
the shoulder masses*

CLASSIFICATION OF THE MUSCLES OF THE TRUNK

Muscles moving the trunk
    Connecting rib cage and pelvis:
        Erector, rectus abdominis, and oblique
Muscles moving the arm
    Connecting trunk with shoulder girdle:
        Rhomboids, levator, pectoralis minor, serratus, and trapezius
    Connecting shoulder girdle with arm:
        Teres major, teres minor, and deltoid
    Connecting trunk with arm:
        Latissimus dorsi and pectoralis major

THE NECK

THE SCALENE MUSCLES. Underlying the superficial muscles of the neck are the scalene muscles. Running between the lateral cervical vertebrae (second to sixth) and the first and second ribs, they buttress the neck and raise the first two ribs during respiration. Though they are almost entirely covered, a small portion is superficial on the lower part of the neck, in front of the trapezius.

THE STERNOMASTOID. We have seen how the trapezius forms the back part of the neck. At the front, the main mass is the sternomastoid. Its name is descriptive of its origin and insertion, as the muscle springs from the sternum and the inner third of the clavicle and is inserted in the mastoid process (just back of the ear). Its two tendons from the sternum are prominent at their origin and mark off between them the hollow called the pit of the neck.

Each tips the head to its own side and rotates it to the opposite side. In rotating, the muscle makes a strong form, as it goes in a direct line between the pit of the neck and its skull attachment (page 117). Together, the two sternomastoids turn the face upward.

The sternomastoid dominates the form of the neck in front

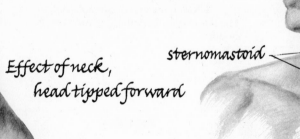

Effect of neck, head tipped forward

sternomastoid

Action of the STERNOMASTOID

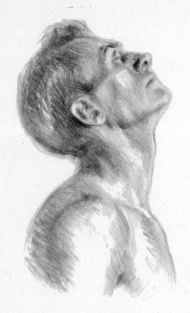

The thyroid CARTILAGE is characteristically prominent in the male & the thyroid GLAND in the female

The sternomastoid is entirely superficial, the clavicular portion blending with that from the sternum as they ascend.

In the inverted triangle formed by the sternomastoids and the boundary of the chin, is the prominence of the *thyroid cartilage* and, below it, the *thyroid* gland. The thyroid cartilage (popularly known as the *Adam's apple*) is prominent in the male; the thyroid gland, in the female. This fact explains the fullness that occurs lower on the neck of the female.

Thin, straplike muscles pass over this portion, but they have little effect upon the appearance, and their detailed description would only complicate the study needlessly.

The change of plane between the under surface of the chin and the front of the neck, is marked by a bone of crescent shape, called the *hyoid* bone. The small muscles forming the under surface of the chin and those passing up from the sternum, clavicle, and scapula connect to this bone and are, for the most part, named for the hyoid bone.[1]

THE PLATYSMA. Over the front and sides of the neck and the upper part of the chest is a very thin sheet of muscle, which changes the appearance of the region when the corners of the mouth are forcefully pulled down. This is called the *platysma* ("flat piece"). In action, it has the appearance of linear ridges converging over the neck toward the corners of the mouth. It shows but rarely—only when there is a condition of great strain. Normally the platysma has no effect upon the fundamental muscles of the neck and the upper chest.

[1] These muscles are sternohyoid, omohyoid, stylohyoid, mylohyoid, and digastric. The last two of these muscles form the floor under the chin. The digastric acts to open the mouth.

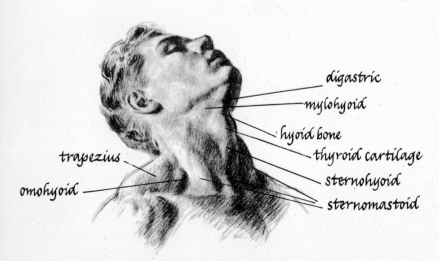

digastric
mylohyoid
hyoid bone
thyroid cartilage
sternohyoid
sternomastoid
trapezius
omohyoid

Plate 31. MUSCLES OF THE NECK

STERNOMASTOID
*from sternum & inner ⅓ of clavicle
to mastoid process*

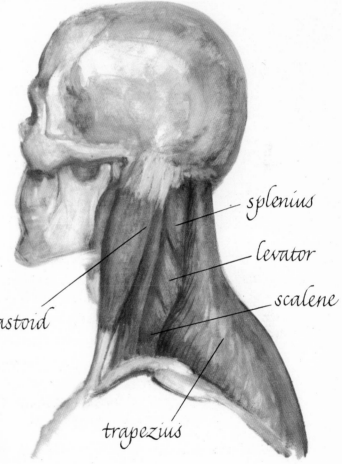

splenius

levator

scalene

sternomastoid

trapezius

SCALENE

*from 1st & 2nd ribs
to cervical vertebrae,
2nd to 6th*

Plate 32. MUSCLES OF THE TRUNK

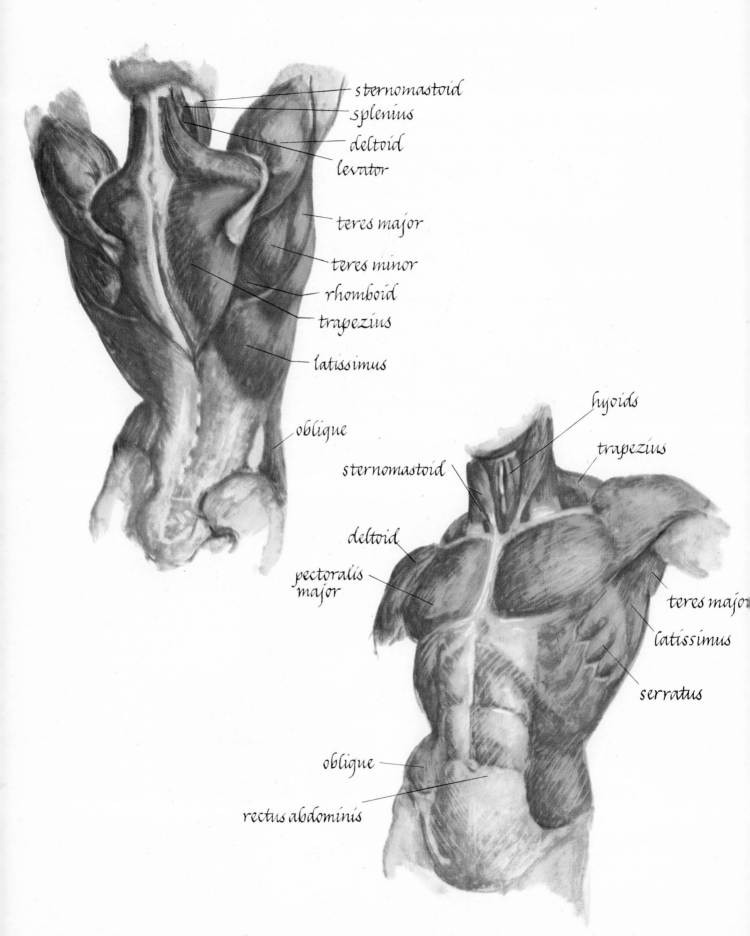

sternomastoid
splenius
deltoid
levator

teres major

teres minor

rhomboid

trapezius

latissimus

oblique

hyoids

trapezius

sternomastoid

deltoid

pectoralis
major

teres major

latissimus

serratus

oblique

rectus abdominis

CONSTRUCTION. The neck is essentially cylindrical, but this form is modified by the triangular planes.

The growth of the neck out of the shoulders and the setting of the head on the neck are great factors in the expression of character and movement.

The head is set well forward on the neck. In the normal position, profile view, a vertical line through the middle of the head runs through the pit of the neck. The axis of the neck slants backward to the shoulders. In front view, but with the head turned, the sterno-mastoid runs almost vertically from the sternum to the skull (page 31).

On the neck, between the sternomastoid and the trapezius, there is an outcropping of the erector spinae (here called the *splenius*), together with parts of the levator of the scapula and the scalene muscles. To discover the various muscles appearing on the surface in their expected places is reassuring. It is like the confirmation that comes from finding the stars in their proper locations in a constellation.

In ordinary action, the shoulders are seldom on a line; but one will usually be higher than the other. Balance requires that the head swing toward the high shoulder.

Guard against weakening the neck. The side boundaries go directly down from behind the ear (page 31).

The relationships between head & neck are keys to character

HEAD & NECK RELATIONS

THE TRUNK AS A WHOLE. To show around the form as far as possible, in Plate 32 the trunk is represented in two three-quarter views; and the muscles have been made to act, by movement given to the figures.

The structure of the skeleton is plainly apparent on the trunk. There is the form of the rib cage, with the line of its costal cartilages, the serratus marking the middle ribs.

Encroachments upon the serratus are made by the latissimus dorsi, which laps over it at the back, and the pectoralis major, which covers its upper portion. The oblique bounds the serratus at the front. It fits with both the serratus above and the latissimus below, its upper four digitations having an origin common to the lower four digitations of the serratus. Its lower four rib digitations fit with those of the latissimus. Above, the shoulder girdle, with its blade bones and collarbones, squares the form of the shoulders, while in back the spines of the scapulae furnish indexes to the movement of the arms. Below are the marks of the hip girdle, whose posterior spines, with the sacrum, form the sacroiliac triangle at the base of the spine. The spinal column is indicated by a groove marking the axis in back, the seventh cervical vertebra being prominent at the base of the neck.

In front, the axis starts with the sternum and is continued by the well-defined linea alba, as far down as the navel. Paralleling this on each side are varyingly depressed points where the abdominis and the oblique join. Lines crossing the front axis are apparent at the clavicles and at the base of the pectoralis. Then there are the three lines in the abdominal region: one at the arch, one at the navel, and one halfway between. And below these is the line joining the iliac crests, besides another uniting the great trochanters. Complementing the abdominal arch below is the round form of the abdomen, bounded by Poupart's ligament.

In this view, the conspicuous bulging masses are the pectoralis majors, the deltoids, and—just above the iliac crests—the obliques. At the pit of the neck, the sternomastoids form their V. Making the shoulder boundary is the trapezius; and at the side, the latissimus appears, with the teres major emerging from it above.

A typical muscular pattern characterizes each view of the trunk

At the side, the serratus supplies its distinctive pattern

The muscles on the front mark off squared forms

The principal masses that constitute the back are the kite-shaped trapezius, the latissimus (thick at the side), and the teres muscles. At the loins are the columns of the erector spinae, whose upper portion —the splenius—is partly superficial, appearing between the trapezius and the sternomastoid.

When the chest is expanded, it presents a quite different appearance from the normal. The familiar muscles have partly disappeared —simplified by being stretched over the rib cage. And now it is the thorax itself that dominates the form. It is thrust upward and outward by the action of the lungs and so stretches the abdominal muscles, as well as the muscles covering it. The result is a flattening of the abdomen and an enlargement of the rib cage, causing a deepening of the chest and a constriction of the waist (page 122).

In back, the trapezius, teres, & deltoids divide the area into triangles

THE HIP

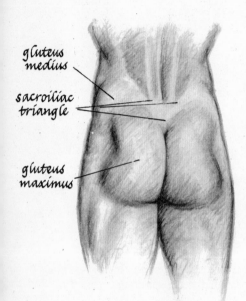

gluteus medius

sacroiliac triangle

gluteus maximus

In back, the trunk appears longer than in front

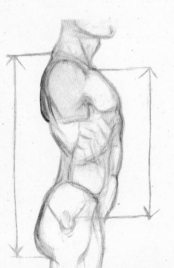

RELATIVE LENGTHS OF TRUNK
IN FRONT & IN BACK

We have seen how muscles running upward from the pelvis form large masses of the trunk and provide the power for moving the column, the rib cage, the skull, and even the arms. Similarly, running downward from the pelvis are muscles which form the hips and the thighs and which act upon the thigh and the leg.

Those forming the hip mass extend, abduct, flex, and rotate the thigh. The superficial parts of this group merge in a broad, tapering band of fascia, or thin connective tissue, which runs down the side of the thigh, attaching to the outer tuberosity of the tibia.

Since it connects the iliac crest with the tibia, this fascia is called the *iliotibial band*.

THE GLUTEUS MAXIMUS. Forming the back mass of the hips are the powerful gluteus maximus muscles. These originate on the back quarter of the iliac crest and along the sacrum. They are inserted in the linea aspera ("rough line") of the femur, and some of their tendons are prolonged to form a part of the band mentioned above. Though the attachment in the linea aspera reaches well down the thigh, the full part of the muscle is at a higher level, and the gluteus maximus appears to end at the base of the hips, or the gluteal fold. This line falls a quarter of a head length lower than the pubis in front, so that the *trunk appears longer from the back*.

The gluteus maximus muscles are powerful. To serve the needs of a being who walks erect, they must be powerful, for they are called upon to raise the trunk to the erect position or to bring the

The gluteus maximus brings the thigh in line with the trunk

bent thigh in line with the trunk. The muscle also acts in rotating the thigh outward.

The gluteus maximus constitutes essentially the whole mass of the hip from the back. Accordingly, it is of primary importance. When the subject stands erect with the heels together, the block form of the mass is roughly square. The individual muscle, however, is bean-shaped. But when the weight is placed on one leg and the other is relaxed, the muscle on the relaxed side is seen to merge softly into the under-thigh muscles (page 140). Plate 33 represents this condition. Because of their full, rounded form, the cleft between the two muscles makes a sharp accent. Naturally the form of the extensive hip muscles is modified by pressure, as in a seated pose, where the weight of the body is placed upon them.

THE TENSOR. Another muscle of the hip that ties into the iliotibial band is the tensor, which comes from the front (page 138).[1]

The tensor originates on the upper iliac spine and runs downward and outward into the iliotibial band. Passing in front of the hip joint,

[1] In Plate 33, showing the tensor, the fascia of the iliotibial band has been cut away to reveal the bony structure.

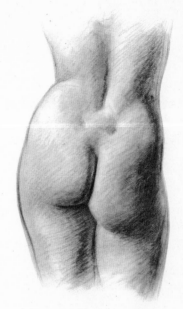

Effect of shifting of the hip, female

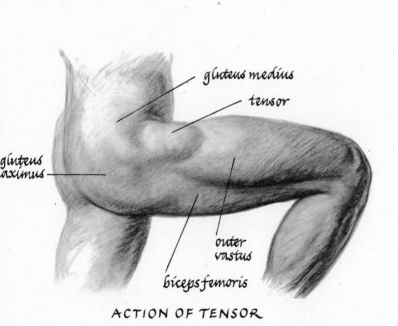

gluteus medius

tensor

gluteus maximus

outer vastus

biceps femoris

ACTION OF TENSOR

Effect of hips in seated figure

it flexes the thigh. It opposes the gluteus maximus in rotating the thigh inward. The tensor increases in bulk near its insertion and, when acting, the muscle makes a prominence between the thigh and the iliac crest, as shown in the illustration.

THE GLUTEUS MEDIUS. Between the gluteus maximus and the tensor is the gluteus medius. Its mass counts with that of the gluteus minimus, a deep muscle, which it covers. The gluteus medius fits, in a V form, between the iliac crest and the great trochanter, to which it is attached (page 114). Thus its action is to abduct,[1] or move the thigh outward, as in the position of "at ease." The gluteus medius is partly covered by the gluteus maximus and also by the fascia, which extends down the side of the thigh to form the iliotibial band. By their connection with this band running to the tibia, these muscles exert a strong influence in supporting the knee. The whole mass of the gluteus muscles and the tensor is superficial.

[1] The terms *abduction* and *adduction* should be carefully differentiated. Abduction, or taking away, refers to the action of those muscles which draw the part away from the mid-line, or axis, of that part. Adduction, the opposite action, means the bringing in of the part toward the mid-line.

The tensor is prominent at the bend of the thigh

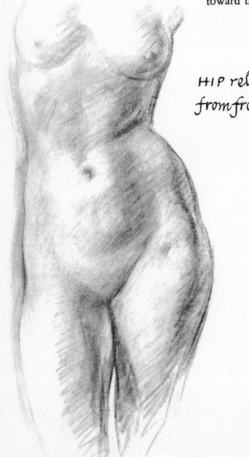

HIP relations from front, female

The gluteus medius abducts the thigh

gluteus medius —

tensor —

gluteus maxim

EFFECT OF GLUTEUS MEDIUS

Plate 33. MUSCLES OF THE HIP

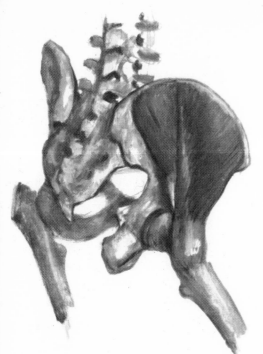

GLUTEUS MEDIUS
abducts thigh
from iliac crest to great trochanter

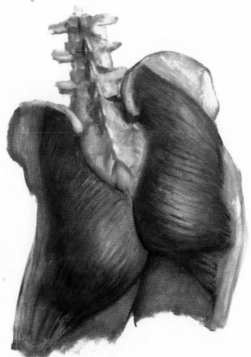

GLUTEUS MAXIMUS
extends thigh on trunk
from back fourth of iliac crest
& sacrum
to rough line of femur
& iliotibial band

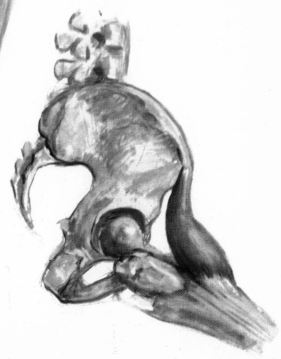

TENSOR
flexes thigh & rotates it inward
from upper iliac spine
to iliotibial band

Plate 34. MUSCLES OF THE HIP

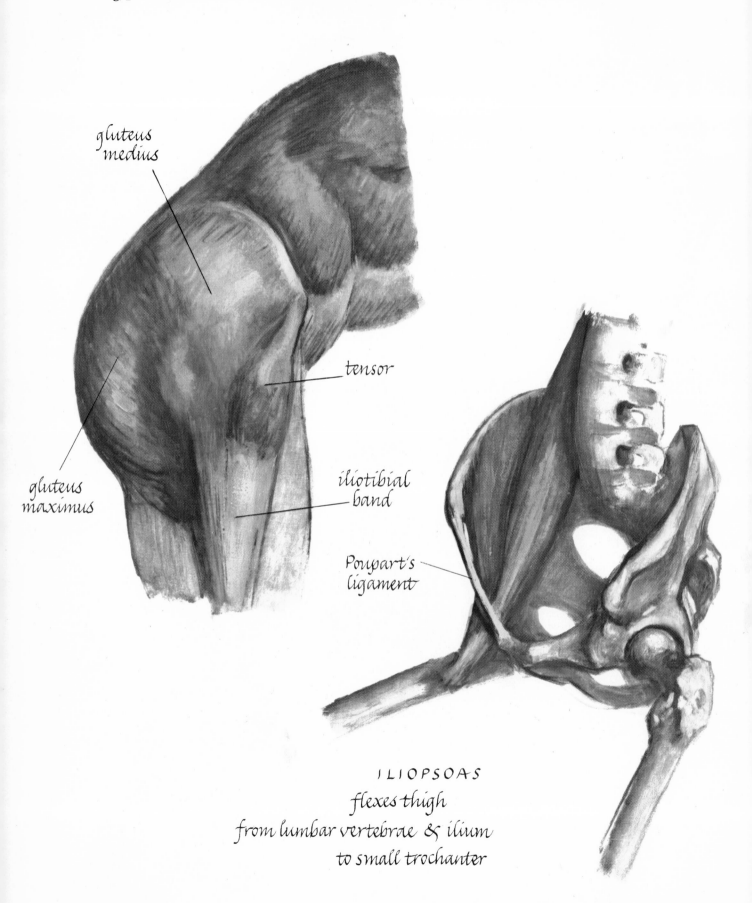

gluteus
medius

gluteus
maximus

tensor

iliotibial
band

Poupart's
ligament

ILIOPSOAS
flexes thigh
from lumbar vertebrae & ilium
to small trochanter

ILIOPSOAS. The most powerful flexor of the thigh is the iliopsoas, which is almost entirely hidden within the pelvis, as it originates on the inner surface of the pelvis and the lateral spines of the lumbar vertebrae (Plate 25, cross section). From this concealed position, the muscle reaches down, converging to its insertion in the small trochanter of the femur.

In its course, the iliopsoas passes beneath Poupart's ligament, or fold of the groin, which forms the lower boundary of the abdomen and so divides the trunk from the legs.

Only on a small area near its insertion is the iliopsoas superficial. It appears in a small triangular area just under the upper iliac spine and Poupart's ligament. The illustration shows the extent and leverage of the muscle as it flexes the thigh.

The concealed iliopsoas powerfully flexes the thigh

COMPARISON OF HIP AND SHOULDER. The structure of the hip region is similar to that of the shoulder. Like the deltoid muscle at the shoulder, the hip mass has its three parts capping the hip. And these converge onto the leg bone, just as the scapular, acromion, and clavicular portions of the deltoid converge on the humerus (Plate 30). Further, the functions of both deltoid and hip muscles are much the same, as they abduct and rotate their respective limbs.

The muscular structures at the hip & at the shoulder are strikingly similar

CROSS SECTION OF THE THIGH

The quadriceps extensor
is the main mass
of the thigh

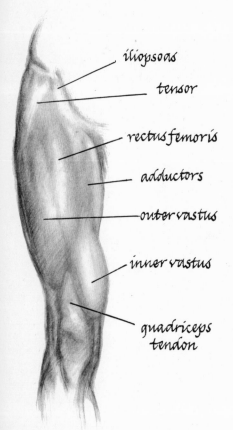

iliopsoas

tensor

rectus femoris

adductors

outer vastus

inner vastus

quadriceps
tendon

THIGH, FRONT, EXTENDED

THE THIGH

The muscles on the thigh, with the exception of the adductors, send their tendons across the knee joint and thus act upon the leg.

EXTENSORS OF THE LEG. On the front and outer side of the thigh, their tendons reaching down over the knee, are the muscles that straighten the leg—the extensors. As indicated in the schematic cross section, this is much the largest of the thigh masses, for a greater force is required to extend than to adduct or to flex the leg.

The extensors are made up of three superficial muscles: the *inner* and *outer vasti* ("large") muscles and the *rectus femoris* ("straight" muscle of the thigh). As there is also a fourth muscle, lying deep, this group is known as the *quadriceps extensor*.

The two vasti originate along the linea aspera ("rough line") on the back of the femur. The rectus femoris originates on the lower iliac spine and is laid over the broader vasti. (It is partly overlapped by the iliopsoas at its origin.) The two vasti and the rectus femoris unite in a common tendon as they approach the knee and, when the mass is acting (leg extended), the joining of muscle and tendon is strongly apparent.

The outer vastus joins the tendon at a much higher level than the inner, which becomes tendinous at the top of the patella. The inner vastus, therefore, accounts for the full form on the inner side just above the knee (page 144). The outer vastus forms the greater part of the outer side of the thigh, extending well back (pages 133 and 180). Its back boundary is well marked in the extended thigh.

The outer vastus
forms most of
the outer side of the thigh

The modeled forms of the rectus femoris as it passes over the vasti produce their subtle variations on the front plane of the thigh (page 179). The rectus is tendinous in its upper and lower quarters and, in movement, shows rhythmic divisions. Incidentally, as the rectus femoris crosses in front of the hip joint, it has the secondary action of flexing the thigh.

The common tendon of the quadriceps extensor carries the patella, to which is appended a ligament for attachment to the shinbone. In this way, the extensors of the thigh have their insertion in the tubercle of the tibia. The action of the patella over the condyles at the knee joint is similar to that of a pulley. In Plate 35, the extensors are shown straightening the leg.

As an exercise, while sitting, extend the leg on a support. Alternately contract and relax the extensors of the leg and note the movements of the ligament binding the patella to the tibia.

FLEXORS OF THE LEG.

At the back of the thigh are the muscles that flex the leg. The semitendinosus and semimembranosus form the inner, and the biceps femoris, the outer mass.

Semimembranosus and semitendinosus. The semimembranosus ("half membrane") and semitendinosus [1] ("half tendon") originate from the ischial tuberosity, together with the long head of the biceps. Thus they cross the back of the hip joint and may act secondarily as extensors of the thigh.

The long tendons of the tendinosus and membranosus go down the lower part of the thigh on the back, inner side and are inserted in the inner tuberosity of the tibia, the insertion of the tendinosus passing to the front. The tendinosus largely covers the membranosus, except at its lower part and on the inner side.

The biceps femoris. Similarly, on the outer side the biceps sends down its tendon to the head of the fibula. As has been mentioned, the long head of the biceps originates on the ischial tuberosity, but the short head comes from the lower half of the linea aspera. Their

[1] The names of these two muscles will hereafter be abbreviated to membranosus and tendinosus, respectively.

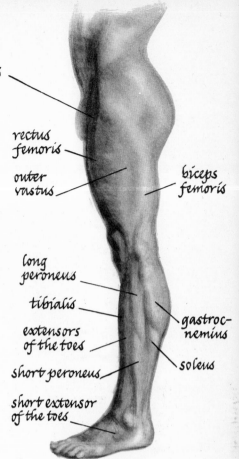

sartorius
rectus femoris
outer vastus
biceps femoris
long peroneus
tibialis
extensors of the toes
gastrocnemius
short peroneus
soleus
short extensor of the toes

EFFECT OF LOWER LIMB, OUTER SIDE

The flexors of the leg form one rounded mass at the back of the thigh

tendons unite, making a straight line to their insertion. They furnish an indicator for the head of the fibula (page 180).

The flexors give the full form to the back of the thigh. When the knee is bent, their tendons are prominent and there is a deep hollow between them—the hollow of the knee. With the knee extended, they appear as depressed lines, the inner line being the deeper, and there is a cross line at the joint, which completes a half H figure. This is particularly apparent in the female.

The tendinosus and the long head of the biceps are superficial, except at their origin, where they are covered by the gluteus maximus.

In Plate 35, the flexors are shown in their action, bending the knee.

The adductors bring the thighs together

ADDUCTORS OF THE THIGH. The adductors of the thigh form the mass high on the inner side of the thigh (page 138). Composed of several muscles that group together, they spring from the surface of the pubis and the ischium. These do not cross the knee joint, but are inserted in the linea aspera. In action, they oppose the gluteus medius in adducting the thigh, *i.e.,* bringing it inward toward the midline, as in crossing the knees. They are superficial in the triangle bounded by the pubis, the inner vastus, and the inner line of the thigh.

SARTORIUS AND GRACILIS. Only two other muscles remain to be considered, in order to complete the study of the muscles situated on the thigh. These two—called the *sartorius* and the *gracilis*

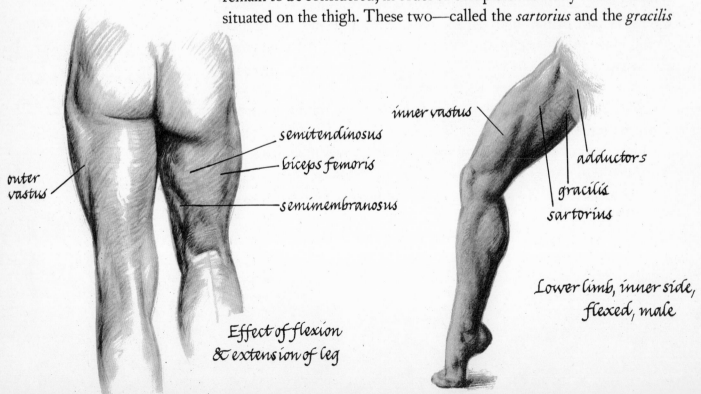

outer vastus

semitendinosus

biceps femoris

semimembranosus

inner vastus

adductors

gracilis

sartorius

Effect of flexion & extension of leg

Lower limb, inner side, flexed, male

Plate 35. MUSCLES MOVING THE LEG

EXTENSORS OF LEG

SEMITENDINOSUS & SEMIMEMBRANOSUS
from ischial tuberosity
to inner tuberosity of tibia

BICEPS FEMORIS
from ischial tuberosity & linea aspera
to head of fibula

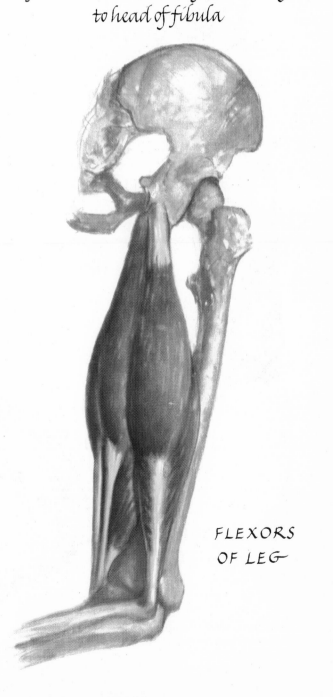

FLEXORS
OF LEG

OUTER & INNER VASTI
from linea aspera

RECTUS FEMORIS
from lower iliac spine

All to tubercle of tibia

Plate 36. MUSCLES MOVING THE THIGH & LEG

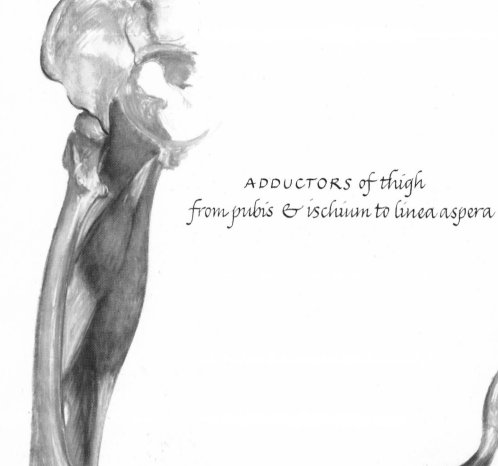

ADDUCTORS of thigh
from pubis & ischium to linea aspera

GRACILIS
from pubis to tuberosity of tibia
Flexes leg & adducts thigh

SARTORIUS
from upper iliac spine
to tuberosity of tibia
Flexes leg
Flexes & abducts thigh

The long sartorius
divides
the thigh obliquely

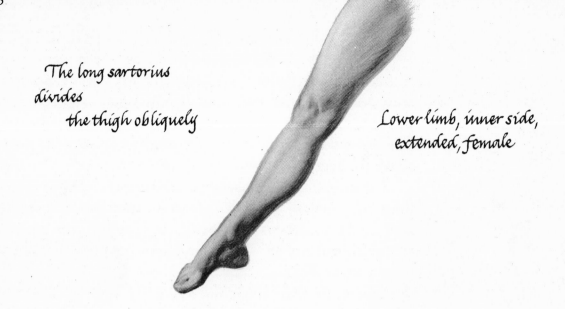

Lower limb, inner side,
extended, female

—have much in common and so will be taken up together. The one more in evidence is the sartorius ("tailor's muscle"), so named because of its prominence when the subject sits cross-legged. It is a long, snakelike muscle, the longest in the body. It runs obliquely across the thigh from the upper iliac spine, taking a sweeping reverse curve and swinging around the inner condyle of the femur to its attachment on the inner tuberosity of the tibia (the same attachment as for the tendinosus).

The gracilis swings down the inner side of the thigh, from the pubis, to attach on the tibia with the sartorius. It, too, takes a double curve on the inside plane of the thigh. The gracilis makes the inner boundary of the thigh from the front. The sartorius marks the division between the extensors and the adductors.

The gracilis unites
with the other adductors
at the inner side
of the thigh

The sartorius, passing in front of the hip joint, acts somewhat as a flexor of the thigh; but both sartorius and gracilis are flexors of the *leg*. The sartorius is an *abductor* of the thigh, while the gracilis, opposing it, acts upon the thigh as an *adductor*. The effect of the sartorius and the gracilis is shown in the drawing of the flexed leg on page 140.

Just below the upper iliac spine, a depression marks the angle between the sartorius and the tensor.

HIP AND THIGH MUSCLES CORRELATED. In Plate 37 the hips and the thigh are shown as they appear in characteristic actions. Occupying the front, is the mass of the quadriceps extensor (the vasti and the rectus femoris), its tendon united to the patella as it crosses the knee to the tibia. In the extended leg, the lower boundary of the muscle is marked by an irregular inverted V above the knee.

Radiating from the pubis are the adductors, the gracilis forming the inner boundary of the thigh from the front. Marking the division between the quadriceps and the adductors, the sartorius takes its long course from the upper iliac spine across the thigh and around the inner knee to the tibia.

Another inverted V appears where the sartorius and the tensor leave their common origin and, at the back, the gluteus maximus and the membranosus show slightly.

The tendons of the sartorius, the tendinosus, and the gracilis can be seen inserted in the inner tuberosity of the tibia. They form a prominent roll, well back on the inner condyle, when the knee is extended; but when the knee is flexed, the conspicuous prominence is on the front, inner part of the knee, where the inner vastus is stretched over the inner condyle (page 60).

The heavy gluteus maximus dominates the form on the back of the hips and the gluteus medius inserts in the depressed great trochanter.

At the back, the biceps sends its tendon to the head of the fibula, while the membranosus and the tendinosus send theirs to the tibia.

The V forms of tendons furnish landmarks on the thigh

The appearance of the knee forms varies with the action

gracilis

inner vastus

rectus femoris
outer vastus

tendons of sartorius, gracilis, & semitendinosus

gastrocnemius

soleus

tibialis

inner malleolus

tendons of flexors of toes

EXTENDED LOWER LIMB, MALE

Plate 37. MUSCLES OF THE HIP & THIGH

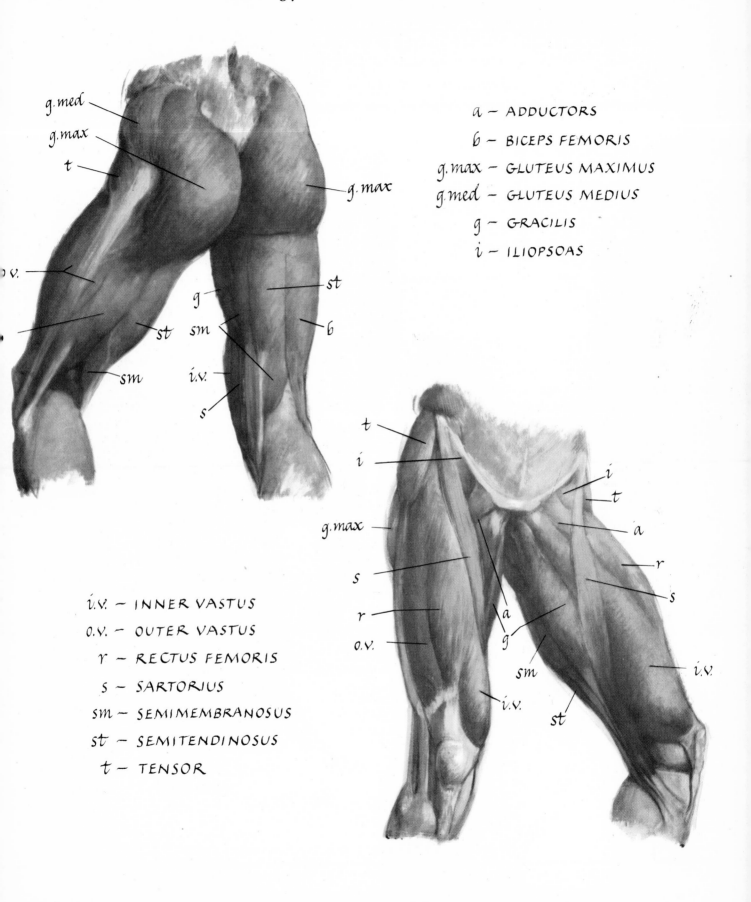

g.med
g.max
t
o.v.
st
sm
g
st
sm
i.v.
s

a — ADDUCTORS
b — BICEPS FEMORIS
g.max — GLUTEUS MAXIMUS
g.med — GLUTEUS MEDIUS
g — GRACILIS
i — ILIOPSOAS

g.max
st
b

t
i
g.max
s
r
o.v.
i
t
a
r
s
a
g
sm
i.v.
st
i.v.

i.v. — INNER VASTUS
o.v. — OUTER VASTUS
r — RECTUS FEMORIS
s — SARTORIUS
sm — SEMIMEMBRANOSUS
st — SEMITENDINOSUS
t — TENSOR

Plate 38. FLEXOR & EXTENSORS OF THE ANKLE

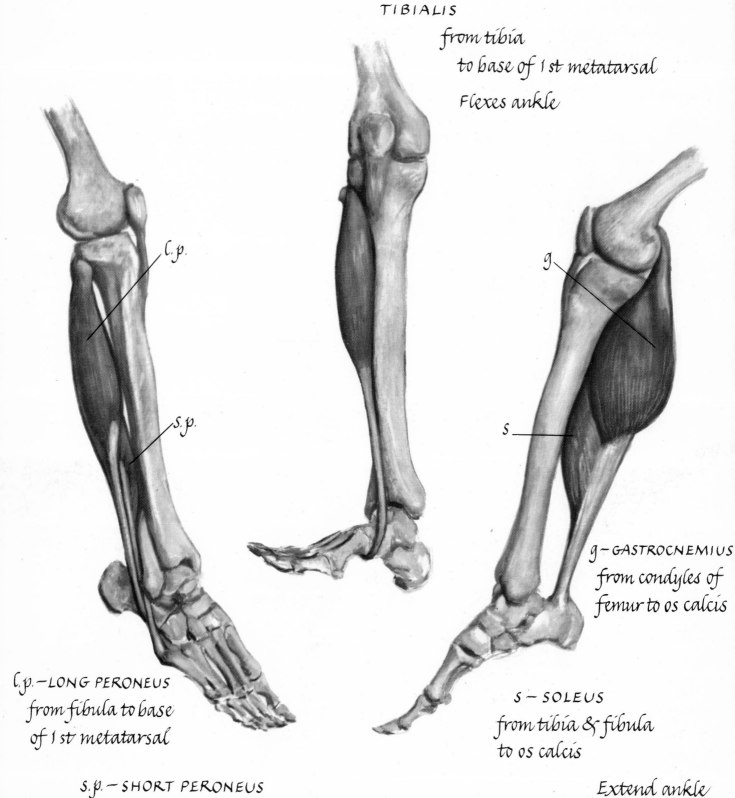

TIBIALIS

from tibia
  to base of 1st metatarsal
Flexes ankle

l.p.

s.p.

g

s

g – GASTROCNEMIUS
from condyles of
femur to os calcis

l.p. – LONG PERONEUS
from fibula to base
of 1st metatarsal

s – SOLEUS
from tibia & fibula
to os calcis

s.p. – SHORT PERONEUS
from fibula to tuberosity of 5th metatarsal
Extend ankle

Extend ankle

Behind the bent knee, a hollow is formed by these tendons; but in the extended thigh, this hollow has disappeared.

On the right thigh, the inner outline is made by the gracilis above, the membranosus and the inner vastus at the middle, and the sartorius below.

CONSTRUCTION. A separation of the thigh muscles is effected by shaking the relaxed limb while standing with the weight shifted. If this is done before a mirror, the division between the several groups of muscles may readily be seen.

The play of lines of the hips and the thigh is most expressive in its rhythms. For constructing them, careful correlation is necessary. The spring of the forms is altered by every shift in the point of view.

The *big form* is what needs to be stressed. The individual muscles of which it is composed should contribute to this form and should never be allowed to break it up.

Work for the BIG FORM

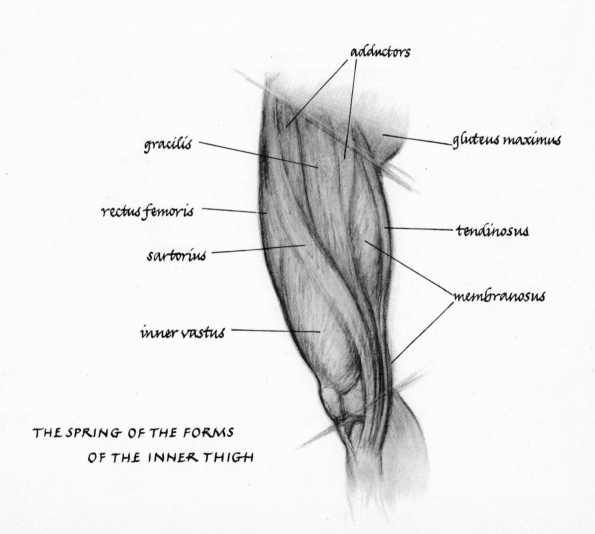

adductors

gracilis

rectus femoris

sartorius

inner vastus

gluteus maximus

tendinosus

membranosus

THE SPRING OF THE FORMS
OF THE INNER THIGH

THE LEG

extensors of toes

tibia tibialis

peroneus

flexors of toes fib.

soleus

gastrocnemius

Cross section of leg

Dominating the front of the shin is the TIBIALIS

Muscles located in the leg operate the foot. They extend and flex the ankle and the toes. The cross section of the leg shows the relative masses.

THE TIBIALIS. At the front is a flexor, the tibialis, which originates along the front, outer side of the tibia. The muscle runs halfway down the shin, where it goes into its tendon. In descending, this tendon swings inward and passes to the underside of the foot, where it is inserted at the base of the metatarsal of the big toe (the first metatarsal). When flexed, the tendinous and the fibrous parts of the muscle are well defined. In Plate 38 the tibialis is shown in its action of flexing the ankle and raising the inner side of the foot.

THE LONG AND THE SHORT PERONEUS. On the side of the leg are the two peronei. The *long peroneus* muscle originates from the head and upper two-thirds of the fibula; the *short peroneus,* from the lower two-thirds of the same bone. On the outer side of the leg, the two muscles form a band, which is broken, a little above the middle, by their tendons. The long overlaps the short peroneus, and their two tendons run straight down the ankle, skirting the outer malleolus and passing to the foot (page 139). The tendon of the short peroneus attaches to the tuberosity of the fifth (little toe) metatarsal, while that of the long peroneus courses into the groove just behind this and passes under the foot, attaching at the base of the metatarsal of the big toe, along with the tendon of the tibialis. Thus a kind of sling is formed under the arch of the foot. The struc-

The peronei form a round band passing straight down the leg

ture aids in the support of the arch and gives strong leverage for extending the ankle and turning the sole of the foot outward.

EXTENSORS OF THE TOES. Between the tibialis and the peronei is a long, slender form, comprising two muscles that extend the toes. These originate along the tibia and the fibula, the extensor of the big toe being a muscle distinct from the extensor of the other toes. Their tendons pass down into the phalanges of the toes and are well defined on top of the foot when the muscle is in action.

As the tendons of the extensors of the toes lie to the front of the outer malleolus and the peronei tendons pass in back of it, the lower part of the fibula is left exposed as a subcutaneous surface.

THE GASTROCNEMIUS AND THE SOLEUS. The largest mass on the leg is at the back, where the powerful calf muscles are located. Upon them falls the burden of raising the weight of the body on the toes. Thus they extend the ankle, as they pull up on the heelbone (page 140).

The mass is composed of the soleus and the gastrocnemius. The soleus is located on the back surface of the tibia and the fibula. It is largely covered in back by the gastrocnemius, which originates *above the knee joint* over the condyles of the femur. The gastrocnemius thus becomes a secondary flexor of the leg. The two bellies start on the upper surface of the condyles of the femur, between the tendons of the tendinosus and the biceps muscles. A more or less distinct line separates the muscles, but in life they appear united in one mass. Just above midway, they join a broad, flat tendon in an inverted V. This is the tendon of Achilles, the strongest tendon in the body. It narrows as it descends, receiving the tendons of the soleus from the sides, and is inserted in the os calcis. The soleus is in evidence all along the outer side of the gastrocnemius, as well as below it on the inner side. The inner border of the gastrocnemius is the more prominent and extends lower than the outer portion. Thus their line of relation opposes that of the malleoli.

As the gastrocnemius has its origin above the knee joint, the ap-

The inner prominence of
the gastrocnemius
is longer than
the outer one

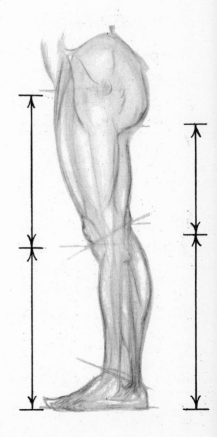

At the back, the leg appears longer
& the thigh shorter than in front

parent length of the leg is greater in back than in front. The thigh is correspondingly shorter in appearance at the back. These points are keys to character in the lower limb.

FLEXORS OF THE TOES. The muscles that flex the toes are placed deeply on the back of the tibia and the fibula and are covered by the soleus and the gastrocnemius. But their lower portions appear briefly on the inner ankle, in the interval between the tendon of Achilles, the back of the tibia, and the soleus. They send down their tendons back of the inner malleolus, then along the groove on the inner side of the os calcis and the arch, to the underside of the phalanges of the toes, from which they act in flexing (turning under) the toes.

The long tendons of the leg muscles are bound firmly to the ankle by broad, flat ligaments, called *annular* ligaments.

SHORT EXTENSOR OF THE TOES. On the outer side of the foot, in front of the outer malleolus, is the short extensor of the toes. It originates at the front of the os calcis and is inserted in the phalanges of the toes, except the little toe. It underlies the tendons from the extensor located in the leg. The muscle lies obliquely on the outer half of the foot and is responsible for the full form in this region.

The flexors
of the toes
are well concealed

The short extensor makes the form
on the foot, to the outer side

Plate 39. FLEXORS & EXTENSORS OF THE TOES

From tibia & fibula
to phalanges of toes

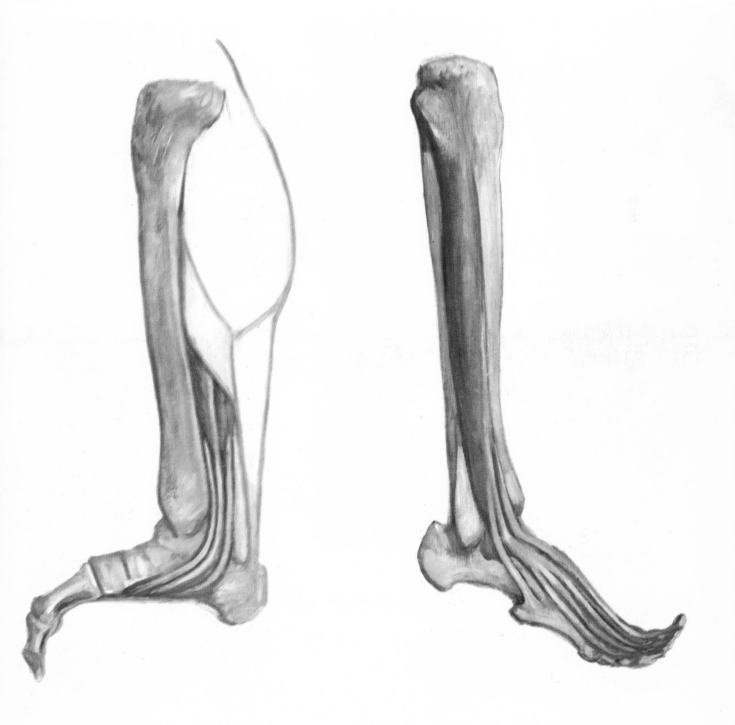

Plate 40. MUSCLES OF THE LEG

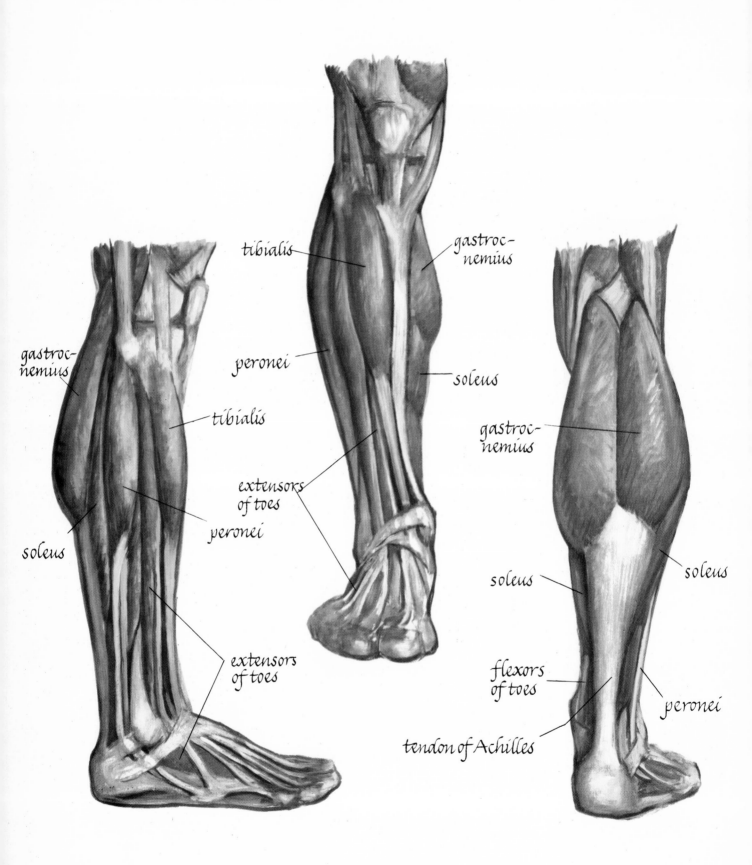

tibialis

gastroc-
nemius

peronei

soleus

gastroc-
nemius

tibialis

gastroc-
nemius

extensors
of toes

peronei

soleus

soleus

soleus

extensors
of toes

flexors
of toes

peronei

tendon of Achilles

THE FOOT

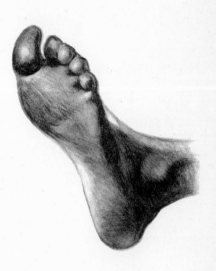

The underside of the foot is provided with concealed muscles (abductors of the toes) and is padded with aponeurosis and covered with extra heavy skin where it makes contact with the ground, *i.e.,* at the heel, the ball of the foot, and the toes. The toes are curved to such a degree that, from the underside, they appear only as pads.

CONSTRUCTION. On top, the four smaller toes arch from the foot, their tips pointing down. The big toe, however, dips and its end points upward.

In drawing, the toes of the foot, like the fingers of the hand, should be *massed* and their details should not be permitted to overshadow the character of the form as a whole. The little toe merely forms part of the outer side of the foot. The only break of importance is between the big toe and the second toe, where a space occurs, back to the webbing between the toes.

This condition is suggestive of the separation between the thumb and the fingers.

Lower extremities, remote from the head, are often drawn out of proportion to it. Therefore, the feet in a figure need to be carefully seen with the head, as well as with the other parts of the figure.

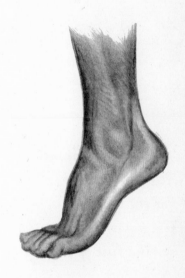

The toes should be massed

CORRELATION OF MUSCLES OF THE LEG. In Plate 40, the muscles of the leg are shown together.

From the front, the fundamental bony form of the knee is preserved, as here the joint is crossed only by ligaments and by the tendons of the muscles located on the thigh. Thus the patella and

The little toe is a part of the outer side of the foot

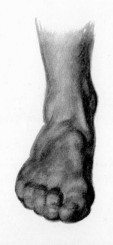

the tuberosities, the tubercle and the head of the fibula, are subcutaneous. The bony structure counts most when the knee is flexed, for then the tendons and the ligaments are stretched tightly over the bones and the fatty tissue. But when the knee is extended, the loose tissue modifies the character of the bony forms (page 60). The whole inner plane of the tibia, including the inner malleolus, is exposed and, on the outer ankle, the malleolus is subcutaneous. The bony structure of the top of the foot, like the hand, is modified chiefly by the tendons that pass across it.

The muscular mass from the front comprises the tibialis, the extensors of the toes, and the peronei, which send their long tendons into the ankle, narrowing the form. The tendon of the tibialis is seen as it disappears under the arch at the base of the big toe. Showing from the back on the inner side, are the gastrocnemius and the soleus. The annular ligament appears as it encircles the ankle, binding down the tendons.

The outer view provides a comparison of the back mass with the muscles of the side and the front. The attachment of the iliotibial band to the tibia and the tendon of the biceps to the head of the fibula may be observed. The profile of the knee slants backward and the tibialis gives a subtle fullness to the line of the upper shin; then it reverses and sweeps forward into the ankle and foot.

The extensors of the toes form a long, slender mass passing in front of the malleolus. Back of them, the two peronei course straight down the leg and in back of the malleolus. In the extended position of the ankle, the muscles of this group stand out individually.

Starting well above the knee joint, the gastrocnemius, with the soleus below, builds the full form of the calf, and their tendon forms the trim back boundary of the ankle.

The hard, round form of the heel, the tuberosity of the fifth metatarsal, and the outer malleolus are the foundational forms of the foot and the ankle in the outer view.

In back, the gastrocnemius, with the soleus beneath it, accounts for most of the form of the calf. Its two heads arise between the tendons of the flexors above and swing downward, the inner head

The inner plane of the tibia is subcutaneous

The peronei, with the extensors of the toes, form the long rectangle on the side of the leg

The gastrocnemius forms the bulk of the calf in back

reaching lower and attaining more fullness than the outer. Thus the line of relation here slants downward and inward, in opposition to the line through the malleoli. In the lower half of the leg, the tendon of Achilles tapers into the os calcis. The long peroneus forms the ankle on the outer side and the flexors of the toes, on the inner. The roundness of the inner border of the knee, compared with the flat form of the outer side, is notable.

SUMMARY OF LOWER LIMB MUSCLES. On the thigh are muscles that move the leg. There are three groups. In front are those muscles which extend the leg—the quadriceps. In back are those which flex the leg—the biceps and the tendinosus muscles. To the inside are the muscles that adduct the thigh and, between these and the quadriceps, is the abductor of the thigh—the sartorius.

There are three main masses on the thigh

On the leg are muscles that move the ankle. At the front is a flexor of the ankle—tibialis. To the outside and at the back are extensors of the ankle—peronei, gastrocnemius, and soleus.

Muscles moving the toes are also lodged in the leg. At the front, outside, is the extensor of the toes, and at the back, lying deep, is the flexor of the toes.

On the foot, outerside, is the short extensor of the toes, while under the sole are abductors of the toes.

On the leg there are muscles that move the ankle & the toes

THE ARM

*The upper limb
has numerous aspects*

The upper limb, with its great capacity for movement, has many aspects. From the shoulder joint the whole limb may be moved backward, forward, upward, and may be rotated. The elbow joint may be bent in different degrees and may twist in turning the hand. The wrist joint bends four ways and also rotates. The 15 joints of the fingers and thumb provide hinge action and some rotation.

*Muscular power
may originate on a region
remote from the part
on which it acts*

The muscles that control the movements of the different parts of the upper limb are stepped down from the parts above. As we have seen, powerful leverage for moving the arm is exerted by muscles coming from the trunk and even from the pelvis. In the same way, muscles that move the forearm originate on the shoulder girdle and the arm. Those controlling the action of the wrist come from the arm, and the muscles operating the fingers and the thumb send their tendons from the arm and the forearm. There are also a few short muscles arising from the wrist, which operate the bones of the hand.

*The biceps
is the typical muscle*

THE BICEPS. The muscle that is perhaps most familiar to people in general is the biceps, lodged on the front of the arm. It is the one displayed by the young boy when the subject is "muscle." It seems to be the symbol of physical strength. This is probably because it is so detached from others as to give it individual emphasis. Also, it is more in evidence and its change of form in contraction is more noticeable than is the change in the case of most muscles. Thus the biceps is the typical muscle (pages 164 and 168).

*The biceps is
a supinator as well as
a flexor of the forearm*

The biceps occupies the front of the arm, toward the inside. Its name (meaning "two-headed") describes its type. The biceps orig-

156

Plate 41. MUSCLES OF THE ARM

BRACHIALIS
*from humerus, lower half,
to coronoid process of ulna*

Flexes forearm

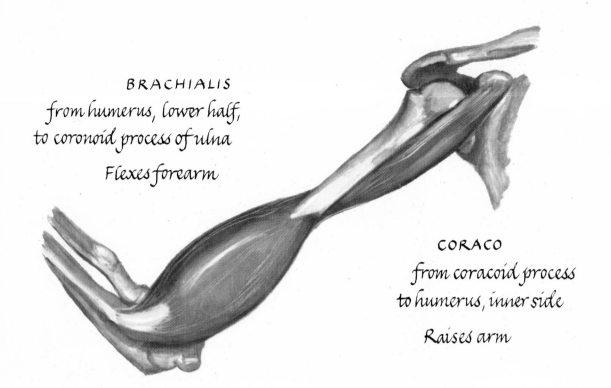

CORACO
*from coracoid process
to humerus, inner side*

Raises arm

BICEPS
*from glenoid cavity & coracoid process
to bicipital tuberosity of radius*

Flexes & supinates forearm

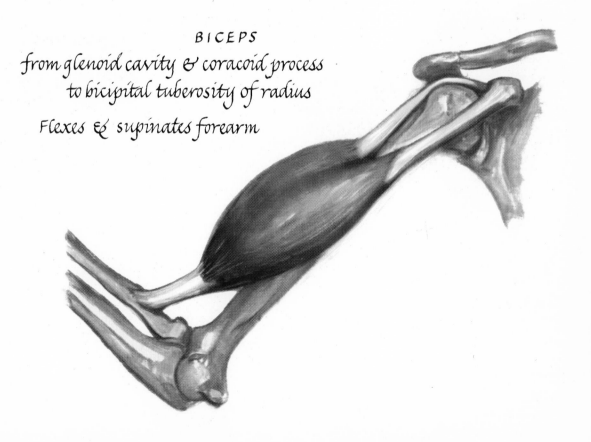

Plate 42. MUSCLES OF THE ARM; ARMPIT

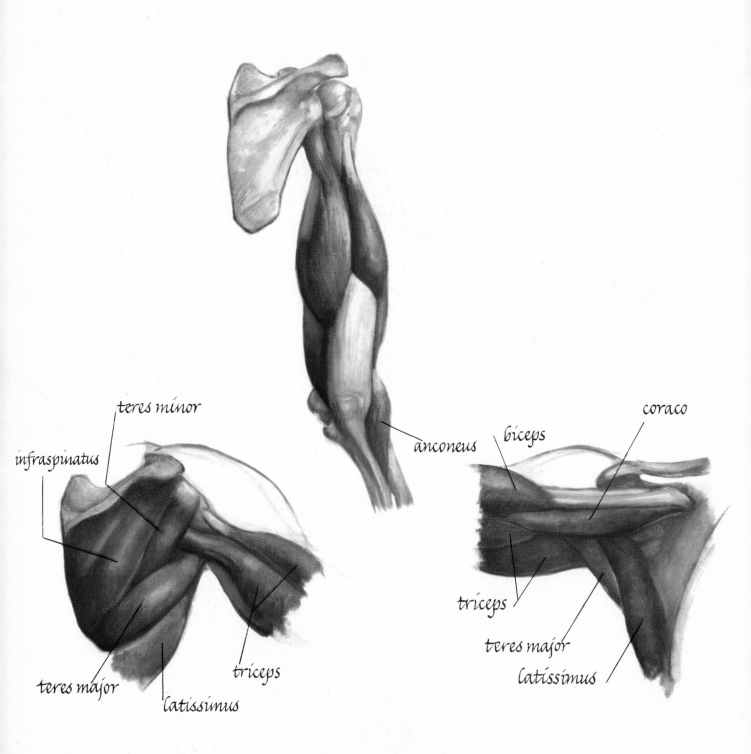

teres minor

infraspinatus

anconeus

biceps

coraco

triceps

teres major

latissimus

teres major

latissimus

triceps

TRICEPS

from humerus & scapula below glenoid

by tendon to olecranon process

Extends forearm

159

inates on the shoulder girdle, the tendon of one head coming from the coracoid process and the other from the glenoid cavity. The tendon from the cavity passes down the bicipital groove. Except for these two tendons, the muscle is superficial. The two parts merge into one soon after their meeting, and the muscle is inserted by tendon into the radius at the bicipital tuberosity. This tendon is prominent when it is under tension, as the muscle acts (page 179).

The biceps flexes and supinates the forearm. Its flexing action is easily observed and the supinating function may be seen if, with the elbow bent, the movements of pronation and supination are made (page 163).

flexion

THE BRACHIALIS. On the lower half of the humerus is the brachialis (from *brachium*, "arm"). It is covered in front by the biceps, but appears on the surface along the outer side and low down on the inside of the arm. As it is attached to the ulna in the coronoid process, the action of the brachialis is limited to flexion of the forearm. In this action, it unites with the biceps. There is, accordingly, a flexor pulling up the forearm by each of its bones: the radius and the ulna.

flexion & supination

The coraco shows only when the arm is drawn out

THE CORACO. The coraco is a small band of a muscle originating on the coracoid process of the shoulder girdle and inserted on the inner side of the humerus. It, therefore, acts only upon the arm, raising it at the shoulder joint and aiding in adduction. Being placed high at the inner side of the armbone, the coraco is hidden from view until the arm is turned outward or raised from the side. It can best be seen when the arm is drawn out, as in throwing (page 179).

THE TRICEPS. The triceps (muscle of "three heads") forms a compact mass and constitutes the form of the back of the arm. Two of the heads originate on the outer and inner sides of the back of the humerus and a third, the long head, comes from the scapula close below the glenoid cavity, passing between the teres

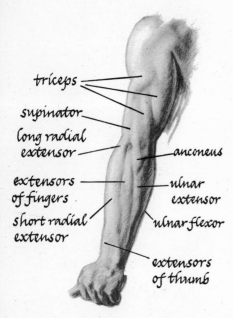

triceps

supinator

long radial extensor

extensors of fingers

short radial extensor

anconeus

ulnar extensor

ulnar flexor

extensors of thumb

The triceps, with its V tendon, determines the character of the back of the arm

The intermuscular septum makes a strong line on the outer side of the flexed arm

minor and teres major muscles. The force to extend the forearm is, therefore, like that of the flexors in front, exerted from two parts: the scapula and the humerus.

About halfway down the arm, the three heads of the triceps join in a common, broad, flat tendon. This tendon is inserted in the olecranon process of the ulna. When acting, the triceps pulls on the upper ulna, straightening or extending the forearm.

The form of the back of the arm is not symmetrical. On the inner side the prominence extends lower than it does on the outer side, a relation like that found in the calf of the leg. The long head of the muscle fits over the upper part of the inner head, but the latter is exposed below. The outer head is almost completely superficial. In the middle of the arm, there is an inverted V, where the triceps joins its tendon. This V is important as a landmark on the arm (pages 72 and 114).

THE ANCONEUS. Extending the leverage of the triceps tendon is a small muscle, called the *anconeus*, because of its location at the elbow. It runs down from the outer condyle of the humerus along the edge of the olecranon. In effect, the anconeus forms a part of the triceps system, but it counts as a distinct muscle at the outer elbow.

INTERMUSCULAR SEPTUM. Down each side of the arm is a wall of fascia, separating the flexors from the extensors. This is called the *intermuscular septum* and, when the arm is flexed, it appears on the outer side as a ridge running upward from the outer condyle. On the inner side the septum from the inner condyle is less conspicuous (pages 159 and 163).

THE ARMPIT. The muscular relationships around the shoulder joint are important to understand, so that one may achieve the correct sequence in the overlappings of the muscles in the different views and actions. The effect of the twistings of the latissimus and pectoralis major have been noted.

The long head of the triceps fits between the opposing teres muscles

Near the axilla, or *armpit*, there is an interlacing of the long head of the triceps with the teres major and teres minor. The long head, coming from the scapula just below the glenoid cavity, is crossed in back by the teres minor, as that muscle passes to its attachment on the back of the humerus. But the long head of the triceps passes in front of the teres major, as the latter goes to its attachment on the front of the humerus.

From the front, the relations are naturally reversed. The teres major is seen as it goes in front of the long head of the triceps. In life, the relations are subtle ones and that is the more reason why one needs to know the character of the structure. For, knowing what to expect, one is able to discover and record those relationships, which are the essence of character in any physical form (page 111).

In Plate 42, the coraco may be seen at the armpit.

ARM AND THIGH MUSCLES COMPARED. There is a striking similarity between the muscular structure of the arm and the thigh. Since the midjoint of the upper limb (the elbow) bends in the opposite way from that of the lower limb (the knee), the structure is reversed, the flexors in the arm appearing on the front and those in the thigh, on the back. The extensors on each are, likewise, oppositely placed. Both groups of arm muscles are of smaller size than those in the thigh, since less force is required to move the forearm than to move the leg. The corresponding groups are also, in part, similarly named.

In the arm, there are three muscular masses originating on the shoulder girdle (two heads of biceps and coraco), just as in the lower limb there are three that originate on the hip girdle (one head of biceps, membranosus and tendinosus). Then there is a muscle—the brachialis—originating on the armbone, which corresponds to the lower head of the biceps of the thigh. Furthermore, biceps and brachialis are connected to both forearm bones, as the flexors of the leg are attached to the two bones of the leg.

At the back of the arm, the three masses of the triceps, inserting in the ulna, compare with the two vasti and the rectus in uniting in

The structures of the arm & the thigh are based upon the same principles

The flexors of the forearm are similar to those of the leg

The extensors of the forearm
& those of the leg
follow the
same scheme

162

a common tendon for their insertion in the tibia. Further, the long head of the triceps, like the inner vastus, attaches to its tendon at a lower point than does the outer head, which corresponds to the outer vastus. As in the thigh mass, there are two parts originating on the limbbone (two heads of triceps) and one overlapping, which originates on the girdle above (long head of triceps). Compare the two vasti and the rectus of the thigh.

Legs and arms, especially the latter, are commonly more poorly drawn than other parts of the figure. The head, more interesting at first and more familiar, though more difficult in its problems, is usually drawn with more character than is any other part. The trunk ranks next in this respect, then legs, arms, and—lastly—hands and feet.

COMPARISON OF STRUCTURE OF ARM AND THIGH

Arm		*Thigh*	
FLEXOR GROUP			
Biceps (two heads)	Originating on shoulder girdle	Biceps (one head) Tendinosus Membranosus }	Originating on hip girdle
Brachialis	Originating on armbone	Biceps (lower head)	Originating on thighbone
EXTENSOR GROUP			
Triceps (three heads)	One from shoulder girdle; two from armbone	Rectus and two vasti	One from hip girdle; two from thigh-bone
ADDUCTORS			
Coraco	Originating on shoulder girdle	Adductors of thigh	Originating on hip girdle

THE FOREARM

Before passing to the two large masses that make up the bulk of the forearm, it would be interesting to examine the superficial muscles that turn the wrist: the pronator and the supinator. Other muscles assist in these actions; but they lie deep, forming one mass with the surface muscles that cover them and, therefore, need no separate study.

THE PRONATOR. The pronator originates on the front of the forearm, at the inner condyle, along with the mass of muscles that flex the wrist and the fingers. It is attached to the outer side of the middle of the radius. Plate 43 shows the muscle contracted, pulling the radius across the ulna. The pronator is superficial, except near its insertion (page 164).

THE SUPINATOR. In spite of its name, the supinator is primarily a flexor of the forearm, though it aids in rotating the radius in the outward direction. It has as its origin the lower third of the outer side of the humerus. The muscle reaches to the lower end of the radius, its tendon being inserted in the styloid process of that bone.

The high origin of the supinator determines the outline of the outer side of the forearm and accounts for the characteristic oblique line of relation between the outer and inner boundaries of the arm at the elbow (pages 164 and 179).

Plate 43 shows the effect of the supinator from the front, as it acts to draw the radius over the ulna from the prone to the supine position.

The supinator gives the full form to the outer side of the arm above the elbow joint

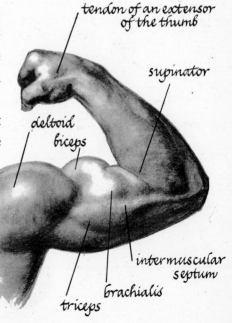

tendon of an extensor of the thumb

supinator

deltoid
biceps

intermuscular septum

brachialis

triceps

UPPER LIMB, OUTER
SIDE, FLEXED

*When the extensors
of the thumb act,
  their tendons show
prominently as they
go out to the thumb*

EXTENSORS OF THE THUMB.
In the illustrations, the muscles of the forearm are shown in their characteristic actions, the flexors bending and the extensors straightening the wrist, fingers, and thumb.

The group of muscles that extend the thumb, though partly covered above by other forms, causes a prominence at the thumb side of the wrist. Originating on the ulna and the radius, they send tendons to the metacarpal and terminal phalanx of the thumb. This group of extensors emerges from between extensor muscles of wrist and of fingers on either side. Two of the tendons of the extensors of the thumb are conspicuous, from the wrist to the knuckle of the thumb when it is extended.

DEEP FLEXORS OF FINGERS AND THUMB.
On the front and inner side of the forearm, the full form is caused by the mass of muscles that flex the wrist. These cover a deep layer of flexors of the fingers and thumb, which are shown in order to explain the flexing of the digits. The muscular portions are lodged in the upper portion of the forearm, and long tendons are sent out to the terminal phalanges of fingers and thumb.

The surface muscles that cover these spring from the inner condyle of the humerus. Their muscular fibers extend about halfway down, where they taper into tendons, which cross the wrist joint.

FLEXORS OF THE WRIST.
On the little finger side, the *ulnar flexor* sends its tendon to the base of the metacarpal bone of the little finger. Balancing this is the *radial flexor*, whose tendon similarly runs to the base of the index finger. Between the ulnar and the radial flexors is the *palmaris*. Its tendon flattens over the palm, where it is inserted in fascia.

The tendons of both deep and superficial flexors show prominently on the wrist as the fingers are alternately flexed and extended.

*The flexors of the wrist
    form ONE MASS
constituting the front of the forearm*

deltoid
biceps
triceps
brachialis
pronator
supinator
radial flexor
palmaris
ulnar flexor
tendons of
deep flexors of fingers

UPPER LIMB, FRONT, EXTENDED

Plate 43. MUSCLES OF THE FOREARM

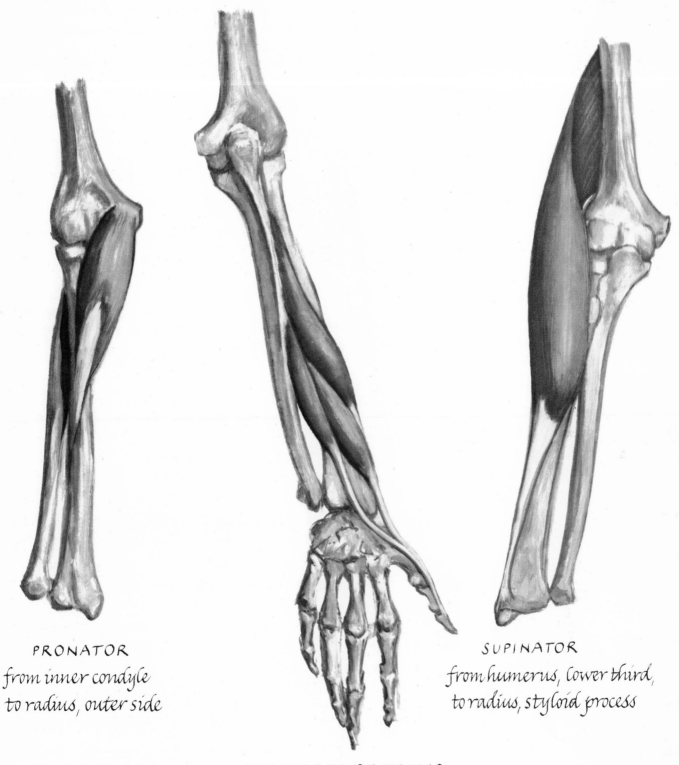

PRONATOR
*from inner condyle
to radius, outer side*

SUPINATOR
*from humerus, lower third,
to radius, styloid process*

EXTENSORS OF THUMB
from radius & ulna to phalanges of thumb

Plate 44. MUSCLES OF THE FOREARM

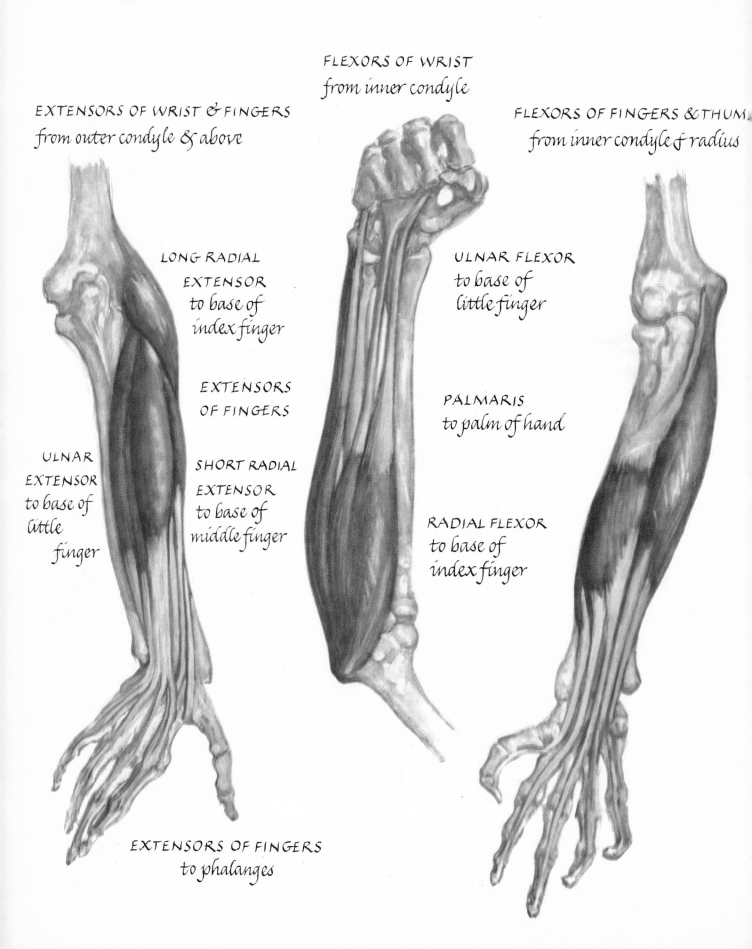

FLEXORS OF WRIST
from inner condyle

EXTENSORS OF WRIST & FINGERS
from outer condyle & above

FLEXORS OF FINGERS & THUMB,
from inner condyle & radius

LONG RADIAL
EXTENSOR
*to base of
index finger*

ULNAR FLEXOR
*to base of
little finger*

EXTENSORS
OF FINGERS

PALMARIS
to palm of hand

ULNAR
EXTENSOR
*to base of
little
finger*

SHORT RADIAL
EXTENSOR
*to base of
middle finger*

RADIAL FLEXOR
*to base of
index finger*

EXTENSORS OF FINGERS
to phalanges

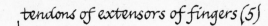

tendons of extensors of fingers (5)

long radial extensor
supinator

extensors of fingers

ulnar extensor

short radial
extensor

FOREARM & HAND
FROM OUTER SIDE, WRIST FLEXED

ulnar flexor

shaft of ulna

EXTENSORS OF WRIST AND OF FINGERS. The extensors of the wrist and the fingers form the mass on the back and outer side of the forearm. The outer condyle of the humerus is their origin, but one, the *long radial extensor* of the wrist, starts somewhat above the outer condyle, grouping with the supinator. This extensor is inserted by a long tendon at the base of the index finger. Below it, the group of three other extensors radiate from the outer condyle (page 114).

Running down along the shaft of the ulna, the *ulnar extensor* sends its tendon to the base of the metacarpal of the little finger.

Thus the long radial and the ulnar extensors conform in their attachments on the *back* of the wrist with the attachments of the radial and ulnar flexors on the *front*. And so there is a flexor and an extensor attached to the base of the radial, or index finger side, and a flexor and an extensor attached to the base of the little finger, or ulnar, side. It is interesting to associate these two pairs, which move the wrist.

The *short radial extensor* has its long tendon inserted at the base of the metacarpal of the middle finger.

Between the ulnar and the short radial extensor are the *extensors of the fingers*. The muscular head runs into a broad tendon, halfway down the forearm. After crossing the wrist, it branches out into several tendons and connects to the phalanges of the fingers.

A flexor & an extensor
are attached to
the bases of the index
finger & of the
little finger respectively

A small, narrow muscle, between the extensors of the fingers and the ulnar extensor, is a special *extensor of the little finger* and adds its tendon to the others.

The tendons of the flexors and the extensors are bound to the wrist by a flat band like a bracelet, which, like its counterpart on the ankle, is called the *annular ligament*.

On the outer side of the forearm, the extensors show rather more distinctly as individual muscles than do the flexors on the front, which form one full, rounded mass.

The supinator and the long radial extensor form the large mass coming from above the elbow; the triceps bounds them at the back and the brachialis, above. In the extended arm, their prominence causes the outer condyle to appear greatly depressed. Below them bulge the other extensors, those of the thumb appearing from between the short radial extensor and the extensors of the fingers (page 114).

deltoid

triceps

biceps

brachialis

The extensors show more individual separation than do the flexors

long radial extensor

flexors of wrist

extensors of wrist & fingers

extensors of the thumb

UPPER LIMB, OUTER SIDE, EXTENDED

THE HAND

As we have seen, muscles that flex and extend the fingers and the thumb are lodged in the forearm. But a number of short muscles that provide for movements between the fingers and between the fingers and the thumb are placed in the hand. These occur primarily on the palm and between the metacarpal bones of the fingers and the thumb.

THE OPPONENS. The opponens of the little finger and the thumb start from the carpal bones at the bases of those digits (the unciform and the trapezium) and from the annular ligament stretching between these bones. They are attached to the outer side of the metacarpals of the thumb and of the little finger. They act to oppose, or bring together, the thumb and the little finger, as shown in Plate 45 and are largely covered by superficial muscles.

The opponens bring together the thumb & the little finger

THE ADDUCTOR OF THE THUMB. The adductor of the thumb originates along the metacarpal of the middle finger and is attached just beyond the knuckle joint on the first phalanx of the thumb. It brings the thumb over toward the palm.

FLEXORS AND ABDUCTORS OF THE THUMB AND OF THE LITTLE FINGER. The thumb and the little finger are furnished also with flexors and abductors. These, with the opponens, make up the mounds on the palm of the hand.

The flexor and the abductor of the thumb and the flexor and the abductor of the little finger, like the opponens, take their origins from their carpal bones; but these *cross the knuckle joints* and are in-

169

The flexors & abductors of the thumb & of the little finger account for the mounds on the palm

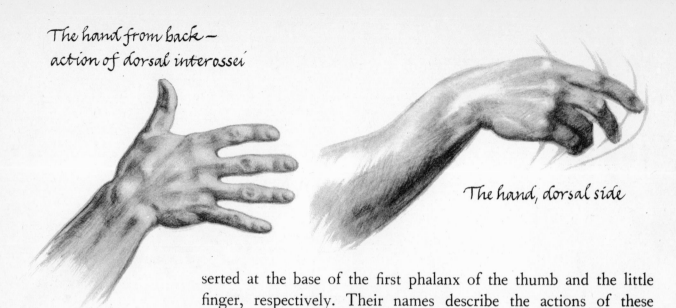

serted at the base of the first phalanx of the thumb and the little finger, respectively. Their names describe the actions of these muscles, which flex and abduct (draw the part outward).

The interossei supply the movements of adduction & abduction between the fingers

THE INTEROSSEI. Filling the spaces between the metacarpals are two sets of muscles, called *interossei* ("between bones"). On the palm side, these are attached to the inner side of the metacarpals of the index, third, and little fingers and cross the knuckle joint for attachment to the first phalanges of these fingers. Their function is to *bring the fingers together* and they are named *palmar interossei.*

Those of the other set are the *dorsal interossei*. Their action is opposite to that of the palmar set, as they act to *spread the fingers*. They originate on the outer sides of the metacarpals of the index and third fingers and from both sides of the middle finger. The first dorsal interosseus has an important surface relationship to the adductor of the thumb, passing in front of the adductor, from back view, and in back of it, from palm view.

CONSTRUCTION OF THE HAND. As has been stated, the construction of the hand is dependent to a very great extent upon the bones. Especially is this true of the back view. The muscles on the palm tend to conceal the bones, and the skin pads over the different segments of the fingers have a like effect. Accordingly, the drawing of the palm view is suggested most readily by elliptical construction.

Observe exactness in relationships

The middle finger is more than half the length of the hand on

Plate 45. MUSCLES OF THE HAND

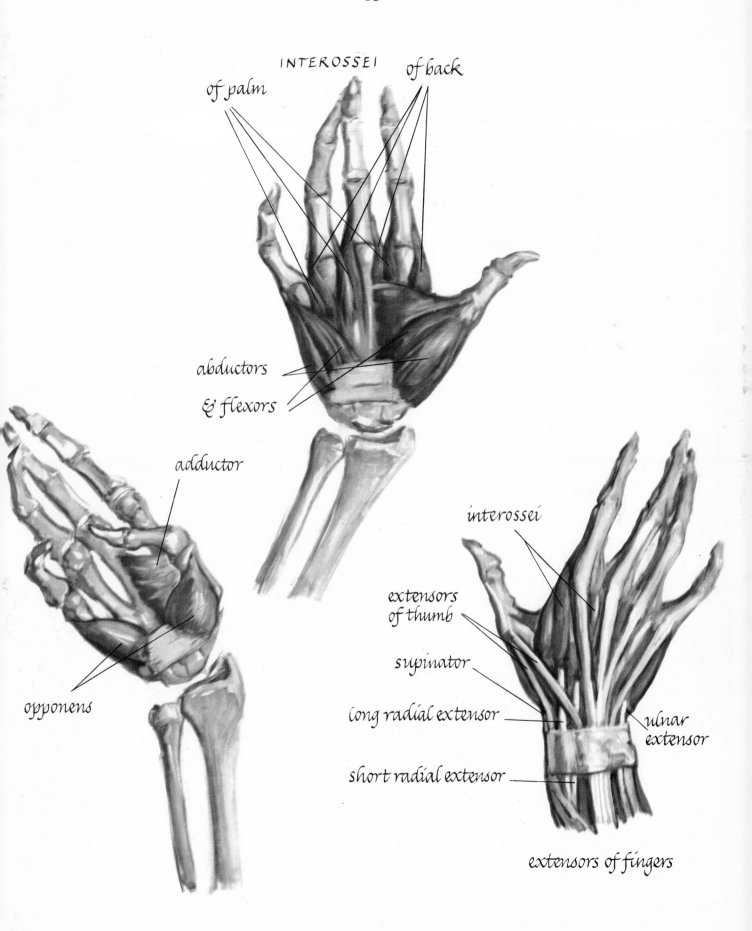

INTEROSSEI

of palm

of back

abductors

& flexors

adductor

opponens

interossei

extensors
of thumb

supinator

long radial extensor

short radial extensor

ulnar
extensor

extensors of fingers

Plate 46. MUSCLES OF THE UPPER LIMB

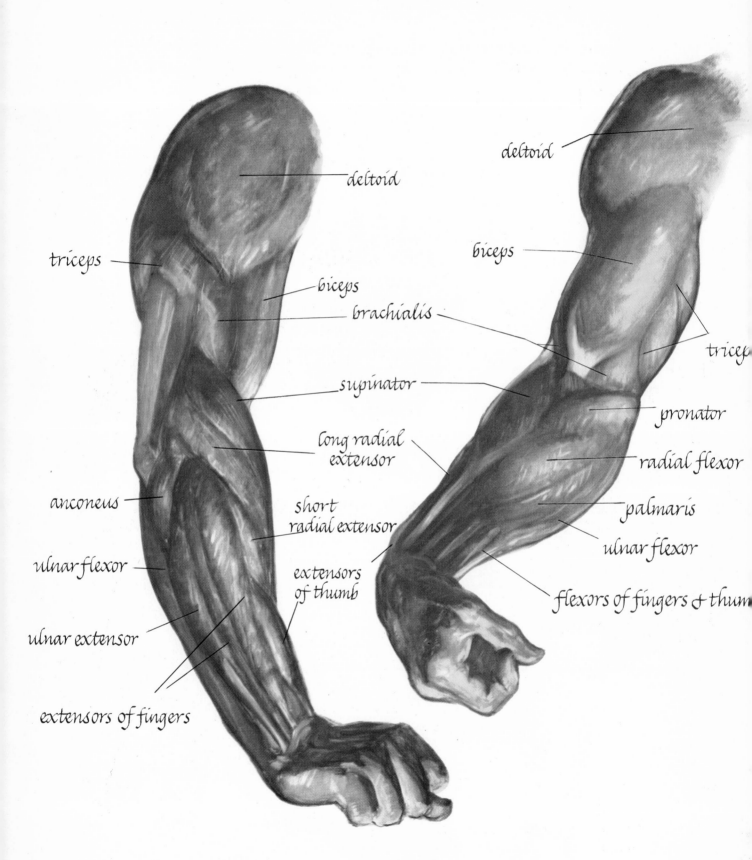

deltoid

deltoid

triceps

biceps

biceps

brachialis

triceps

supinator

pronator

long radial extensor

radial flexor

anconeus

short radial extensor

palmaris

ulnar flexor

ulnar flexor

ulnar extensor

extensors of thumb

flexors of fingers & thum

extensors of fingers

the dorsal side but less than half on the palm side, the reason being that the fingers appear to end at the webbing on the palm. A glance at the fingers in profile will show that the crease corresponding to the webbing occurs halfway up to the middle joint. The relations of all the other creases to their joints are important to observe, so that the character of the fingers may be expressed.

There is always a focal point on the hand, often the middle knuckle. If the fingers are together, it is necessary to see them *as a mass* and not as single forms separated by black outlines. From the back, the creases between the fingers all point *away* from the axis, which runs through the middle finger. To maintain the organization of the hand, it is necessary to keep in control divisions between fingers, which should be suggested rather than drawn. There may be but one accented line to give the complete idea. The thumb always opposes the fingers. In the extended hand, when the fingers are in back or in front view, the thumb is seen in three-quarter view. When the fingers and the hand are seen from either side, the extended thumb is in full front or back view.

Well-constructed hands are the exception, because the draughtsman too often becomes impatient with them and will not take the trouble to coordinate their parts. Yet the hand is tremendously important. In practice, the hand ranks next to the head as the most important part of the figure. Heads and hands are much more often in full view than are the other parts of the figure. With the head, the hand expresses the character of the individual, and the hand varies in type as much as does the head.

Students usually believe that hands and feet are more difficult to draw than other parts of the anatomy. The reason for this opinion is their common unfamiliarity with the extremities, owing to lack of study. A great many times more heads than hands and feet are drawn

The webbing of the fingers occurs halfway between the knuckles & the middle joint

The fingers should be considered AS A MASS

The hand, palm side, thumb extended

*The hand is constructed
upon principles
similar to those used
for drawing the head*

by art students. This absorption with heads implies a slighting of hands and feet.

As a matter of fact, the hand is much more simple to construct than is the head. As soon as the anatomy of the parts and the principle of construction are understood and applied in practice, it will be realized that there is nothing in the structure of the foot or the hand to make it any more of a problem to represent than any other part of the figure.

SUMMARY OF THE UPPER LIMB MUSCLES.

*The muscles
on the upper limb
are stepped down
from the part above*

On the arm are muscles that move the forearm. At the front are those which flex the forearm: the biceps and the brachialis, while on the back are the triceps, which extend the forearm.

On the upper half of the forearm are muscles that move the wrist through their long tendons.

In front, coming from the inner condyle, is the flexor group and underlying the flexors of the wrist are flexors of the fingers and the thumb.

In back, coming from the outer condyle and above, is the extensor group. Between the extensors of the wrist are the extensors of the fingers and the thumb.

On the palm side of the hand are grouped the small muscles that oppose, abduct, adduct, and flex the thumb and the little finger.

Between the bones of the palm are the muscles that separate and bring together the fingers.

MUSCLES OF THE UPPER LIMB CORRELATED.

*The deltoid determines
the form of the shoulder*

In Plate 46, the drawing presenting the outer side of the arm shows, in action, the muscles that extend the wrist.

The powerful deltoid appears tucked in between the biceps and the brachialis. To the back of the latter, the triceps are seen running into their tendon.

The upper forearm mass (the supinator and the long radial extensor) appears in front of the triceps on the lower third of the hu-

*On the outer side, the forearm mass
begins well above the elbow joint*

merus. The other extensors radiate over the side of the limb as they swing down from the outer condyle.

Between the short radial extensor and the extensors of the fingers emerge the extensors of the thumb. And beyond the shaft of the ulna, a part of the ulnar flexor can be seen.

When they are in action, the extensors are individually discernible.

On the front, the biceps, bulging from under the deltoid, dominates the arm. The brachialis shows each side of it below, and two heads of the triceps make the inner plane.

The biceps dominates the front of the arm

The flexors of the wrist form one mass as they come from the inner condyle, along with the pronator. To the outside appear in order the supinator, the long radial extensor, and the extensors of the thumb. The tendons of the flexors are prominent on the front of the wrist when it is flexed.

The flexor tendons are prominent when the wrist is flexed

CONSTRUCTION OF THE UPPER LIMB. In the extended position, feel the swing of the *entire limb at once* as you take your lines from the shoulder all the way down into the fingers.

Locate the elbow and wrist joints with cross lines.

Make the first lines FOLLOW THROUGH

There is an unsymmetrical balance as the full forms oppose each other. The deltoid dominates the shoulder region. Emerging from under it in a long cylindrical form on the front is the biceps.

The supinator and extensor mass contributes its form to the upper elbow. This is opposed by the flexor mass, lower down on the inner side. In the normal position—front view extended—the limb is alternately broad, narrow, and broad. Through the biceps, we see the form in its narrow view; but from the elbow section down, it is the broad side that is presented (page 164). There is less variation when the limb is in the position of pronation. The tendons taper into the wrist, which is reinforced on the thumb side by the thumb extensors (page 168).

The flexed upper limb is alternately broad, narrow, broad

In the flexed limb, the forms on the outer side are full. Therefore, the line of the outer side of both arm and forearm will be *convex* outwardly (page 159).

Around joints such as wrist and elbow, the hard tendons, when taut, make a strong transition between muscle and bone. This needs to be watched for and emphasized.

Watch for the *outcropping of the bones* at the elbow, wrist, and finger joints.

Tendons, when taut, make conspicuous transitions between muscle & bone

ACTION

The full effect of the muscles of the body is, of course, best seen in strong action. Most studio poses, however, are necessarily quite relaxed, as it is manifestly impossible for the model to hold strong action for any length of time. Study of this type, then, must be done largely from memory and imagination; and an understanding of the bones and muscle is a prerequisite for such work, as it is always imperative that the parts be correctly related and the accentuations be properly placed. Photographs are an aid if they are not *depended upon*.

Most actions fall under one of the following classifications or some combination of them.

Effect of extension

Rhythm of the figure

CROUCHING ACTION

It will be recalled that the first principle of action is illustrated, in a stationary figure, by a *shifting of the weight* of the body so that it is borne unequally by the feet. The relaxed standing pose exemplifies this action, in which rotary, as well as tilting, movements between the head, shoulders, and hips are most expressive of life (pages 16, 17, and 18).

A second condition of action is the introduction of an *artificial support*. Examples would be presented by a figure sitting, leaning, crouching, reclining, swimming, using a staff, engaged in certain gymnastics, and the like (pages 123 and 133).

ACTION IS DETERMINED BY SEVERAL FACTORS:

1 Shifting of the weight

2 Use of an artificial support

3 Introduction of a weight
   external to the body

4 Force of movement by which
   dynamic balance is maintained

EFFECT OF TWISTING MOVEMENT

A third condition affecting action is the introduction of a *weight external to the body,* as in a figure carrying a load or using an implement in some manner. Many examples of this type of action may be found in athletics. Baseball, golf, tennis, field events in track, basketball, football, wrestling, hockey, etc., all furnish numerous examples of this form of action or a combination of it with any of the other conditions.

DYNAMIC BALANCE
WITH WEIGHT

ACTION, AS WITH WEIGHT

DYNAMIC BALANCE
THROUGH FORCE OF MOVEMENT

A fourth condition of action is that in which *dynamic balance is maintained through force of movement,* as in a figure *in motion*—walking, running, dancing, leaping, diving, and the like. In such actions the synchronized movements of the arms and legs and of the shoulders and hips, acting in opposition, create the force of the rhythm.

CONSTRUCTION. To make the action figure go together, the first line should be swung in and go *all the way through*. This should express the action. Then keep relating the parts by working all over the figure constantly, never dwelling on any one portion until after the *form as a whole* has been established.

The quality of movement is suggested in a subtle way by line. The play of light and shade over the form produces rhythm in pattern, an expedient that is also of great use when expression of positive form is desired.

*There should be
no break in the rhythm*

DYNAMIC BALANCE,
WITH ARTIFICIAL SUPPORT

DRAPERY

In the draped or costumed model, there is the same necessity to know the anatomy of the figure as in work from the nude, for drapery is so intimately associated with the figure that it becomes an integral part of the study of anatomy.

Like all other things, drapery has form of its own; but a piece of drapery or an article of clothing hanging by itself is one thing and the same material worn by a person is another—and a quite different—thing.

A draped or costumed figure is still essentially a figure. The covering fits over the form, but is subordinate to it (except, perhaps, in fashion design, where the important item is the clothing). Accordingly, the problem must still be primarily one of drawing the figure. The practicing artist may be confronted with the necessity of drawing a figure that is wearing anything, from a loincloth or a pair of bathing trunks to a suit of armor. Any material placed over a form follows that form.

Drapery is subject to mechanical laws. The general principle of drapery is that it is held at some point, from which it drapes more or less freely depending upon conditions. Drapery follows the form that is supporting it and then hangs free. A bent thigh, elbow, or knee produces tension over the flexed joint where the material is tightly drawn. Contrasting with this is the repose on the side opposite the tension point. Here the drapery organizes itself in rhythmically radiating folds, of varied pattern. No two coat sleeves, for example, exhibit the same system of folds.

It is at the tension and the suspension points that the anatomical forms of the figure are apparent. Where it is free, the drapery breaks

Drapery is subordinate to the form

Drapery is subject to mechanical laws

Drapery has an ornamental function

the form. Thus drapery has the ornamental function of modifying the human figure, now revealing, now concealing, now simplifying, now embellishing the form.

Drapery can obscure the form as, for example, in the heavy, loose robe worn by a bather. Also it may confuse the form, as when a sheet is loosely draped over a reclining figure, its numerous transverse folds cutting across the form.

Heavy material falls in only a few simple folds, while lightweight material takes many. The character of the folds varies also with the texture. If the material is crisp, like a man's linen shirt, it wrinkles in a different way from silk. So every material has a quality of its own—a quality that identifies it. Examples are everywhere.

The important thing is to *assure character in the folds*. This is a matter of getting variety in their shapes, sizes, and directions, and then treating them broadly and simply, so that they will not assume more importance than the figure itself.

A system of organizing the folds has to be devised—one that will be interesting because movement of the particular material draped on a particular form is well expressed. That is good design.

To the subject of drapery belongs the fitting to the form of anything that is worn. A hat has to be constructed with the head; a string of beads, with the neck; a slipper, with the foot. Whether they are tight or loose fitting, all articles of wearing apparel should be drawn *with the form*—not the form drawn first, with the apparel added afterward.

The clothing that has the most anatomy is the clothing that has been worn a long time without pressing. Old shoes and even gloves retain the character of the form after they are taken off. An old pair of trousers, even when hanging on a hook, will suggest the legs of the wearer. Along the same lines, drapery or clothing that is wet (especially if it is thin) clings to the form and thus reveals it much more completely than it would if dry.

Classical drapery is effective because it is simple, draping naturally over the form and preserving, while veiling, its fine contours. Good costume design should be a constructive agent, complementing

The effect of the folds is determined by the drapery material

Variety is needed to give character to the folds

Anything worn should be constructed WITH THE FORM

the form. But mere fashion design is not always artistic. It is often grotesque, appealing only to a taste for novelty. Often—intentionally or unintentionally—its effect has been even to deform the figure; or, if it does the figure no positive harm, it is likely to be merely a covering, like present-day men's suits.

The collar of a man's shirt or coat should be drawn *to fit over the neck*. Such an admonition may seem superfluous, but collars in drawings too frequently appear to cut into, instead of to fit around, the neck. Ties, likewise, should have their quota of character. Nothing is too unimportant to be well designed.

Anything that simplifies the form contributes to its beauty. A veil over a woman's face is invariably flattering. Not only does it suggest exclusion and make the face seem more precious; but, at the same time, it simplifies the contour—pulls the face together, so to speak.

Simplicity is a valuable quality in drapery

CONCLUSION

Systematic drawing practice is a necessity

No book can *give* you the ability to draw the figure. Only *you* can achieve that by constant practice, both from life and from imagination. It cannot be attained by a few superficial tricks or by formulas.

This volume is a guide. It illustrates and explains the essential structure of the figure and the principles of construction, which, if thoroughly studied and applied, will yield the understanding required to do good work. Not only technical excellence but the cultivation of discriminating good taste is the aim.

Complete directions for study, including many points not covered heretofore, are provided. All the essential material is here and is in simplified form. Superfluous matter has been excluded.

For an art student, for practicing artist, illustrator, sculptor, art educator—for all who are interested in the character and functions of the muscular and bony structure of the figure—this book supplies the requisite material for reference.

All essential material for study & for reference is provided

GLOSSARY

Abdominal arch. The arch formed by the rib cartilages as they ascend from each side and join at the pit of the stomach.

Abdŭc'tion. The act of drawing the part *away* from the axis or midline of the body.

Abdŭc'tor. A muscle whose action is outward, away from the body.

Achilles, Tendon of. The tendon connecting the large muscles of the calf with the heel-bone; named from the Greek hero, Achilles.

Acrō'mion process. The outer portion of the spine of the scapula, forming the cap of the shoulder.

Addŭc'tion. The act of drawing the part *toward* the axis or midline of the body or part.

Addŭc'tor. A muscle whose action is to draw inward toward the median line, or axis, of the body.

Anconē'us. A small triangular muscle located at the outer elbow.

Annular ligament. The flat band that passes around the wrist or the ankle to hold in place the tendons crossing the joint.

Aponeurō'sis. Thin, flat tendinous material covering and forming terminations of some muscles.

Arm. That part of the upper limb between the shoulder and the elbow, as opposed to the forearm.

Articulation. A joint between bones in the skeleton.

Axilla (ăk-sil' à). The armpit.

Bī'ceps. Two-headed. A muscle on the front inner side of the arm, which flexes the forearm. It derives its name from its two-headed form.

Bī'ceps fĕm'oris. The two-headed flexor of the leg located on the back of the thigh.

Bīcip'ital groove. A groove on the front of the humerus in which is lodged a tendon of the biceps muscle.

Brāchiā'lis. A muscle on the lower front part of the arm, which flexes the forearm.

Bŭc'cinātor. A muscle of the cheek, between the jaw and the face.

Căpitĕl'lum. The rounded prominence on the lower end of the humerus by which the humerus articulates with the radius.

185

Căr'pal. The eight bones of the wrist, which form the transition between the radius and the bones of the hand. They are named for their forms.

Cer'vical. Pertaining to the neck, as the cervical, or neck, vertebrae.

Clăv'icle. The collarbone. The collarbones form the front part of the shoulder girdle.

Coccyx (kŏk' siks). The several small vertebrae forming the tip of the spine. The mass is named from its resemblance to a cuckoo's beak.

Common extensor of the fingers. A muscle located on the back of the forearm whose tendons run to all the fingers, but not to the thumb.

Compressor. A muscle of the nose. Its action is to contract the nostrils.

Cŏn'dyle. A prominence closely associated with the articulation of a joint.

Cŏr'aco. A small muscle originating at the coracoid process.

Cŏr'acoid. A prominence on the upper scapula, occurring just below the clavicle; named from its resemblance to a crow's beak.

Cŏr'onoid. One of the small processes on the mandible or the ulna. Also the name of a shallow depression on the lower humerus, the coronoid fossa.

Cŏr'rugator. A small muscle that contracts the brows.

Cŏs'tal. Pertaining to the ribs, as costal cartilages.

Cū'boid. A tarsal bone located on the outer side of the foot; named from its square form.

Cŭnē'iform. Wedge-shaped. One of the three tarsal bones forming the arch of the instep. Also a carpal bone on the ulna side of the wrist.

Dĕl'toid. From the Greek letter, delta, triangular. The muscle forming the pad of the shoulder.

Deltoid impression. A roughened ridge nearly halfway down on the outer surface of the shaft of the humerus, for the insertion of the deltoid.

Deprĕs'sor. A muscle that draws down the corners of the nose or the mouth.

Dôr'sal. Referring to the back of a part. The region of the back between the neck and the loins.

Ĕrĕc'tor spī'naē. The long, deep, extensor muscle of the back. An erector muscle is one that straightens or keeps a part erect.

Extĕn'sor. A muscle that extends or straightens a joint.

Facial angle. The angle made on the profile skull by the intersection of the axis of the face with the axis of the skull.

Fascia (făsh' ĭ-à). A sheet of tissue covering or binding together structures of the body.

Fē'mur. The thighbone, longest and strongest bone in the body.

Fĭb'ula. The long, slender bone at the outer side of the leg, whose lower extremity forms the prominence on the outer side of the ankle.

Flĕx'or. A muscle that bends a joint.

Floating ribs. The two lowest ribs, eleventh and twelfth, which are not connected with the sternum.

Forearm. The part of the upper limb between the elbow and the wrist.

Fŏs'sa. A shallow cavity or depression in a bony part.

Frontal bone. The mass of bone forming the forehead.

Frontal eminence. One of the two prominences on the upper, outer portion of the frontal bone.

Găstrocnē'mius. The large, superficial muscle forming the main bulk of the calf.

Glē'noid cavity. The shallow cavity in the scapula for the articulation of the humerus.

Glutē'us măx'imus. The two powerful muscles forming the back of the hips, which extend the thigh.

Glutē'us mē'dius. The middle muscle on the side of the hip, which abducts the thigh.

Gracilis (grăs' ĭ-lĭs). The long, slender muscle of the inner side of the thigh.

Great trŏchăn'ter. The rough prominence at the upper end of the femur.

Hip girdle. The bones of the pelvis, which encircle the hip region and furnish attachment for the thighbones.

Hū'merŭs. The armbone.

Ĭl'ĭăc crest. The ridge forming the upper boundary of the ilium bone of the pelvis.

Ĭl'ĭăc spine. One of the two prominences on the front border of the ilium.

Ĭlĭŏfĕm'oral ligament. An inverted Y-shaped ligament running from the upper iliac spine to the upper end of the femur. It aids in keeping the figure erect.

Iliopsoas (ĭl-ĭ-o-sō' ăs). The powerful flexor of the thigh coming from inside the ilium and the lumbar vertebrae to attach to the lower iliac spine.

Ĭl'ĭŏtĭb'ial band. A flat tendinous strip on the side of the thigh, giving connection between the gluteus and tensor muscles of the hip and the tibia.

Ĭl'ium. One of the large upper bones of the pelvis, whose crest is the top border of the hip girdle.

Infraspīnā'tus. A muscle located on the scapula below its spine and grouping with the teres minor.

Inner văs'tus. The great muscle of the inner thigh, forming part of the quadriceps extensor of the leg.

Interŏs'sēi. Small muscles lying between or beneath the metacarpal bones of the hand or the metatarsals of the foot.

Ischial (ĭs' kĭ-ăl) *tuberosity*. The tuberosity on the ischium bone of the pelvis.

Ischium (ĭs' kĭ-ŭm). One of the ring-shaped bones on the under part of the pelvis, which bear the weight of the body in the sitting position.

Lătĭs'simus dôr'sī. The broad, flat superficial muscle covering approximately the lower half of the back.

Leg. That part of the limb between the knee and the foot, as opposed to the thigh.

Levā'tor. A muscle that elevates, as levator of the scapula. Also certain muscles of the quadrate group.

Lĭg'ament. A tough band of tissue serving chiefly to bind together the bones.

Lĭ′nea ăl′ba. The "white line," a tendinous furrow corresponding to the axis of the trunk, from the sternum to the navel.

Lĭ′nea ăs′pera. The "rough line," or ridge, extending down the back of the femur.

Long radial extensor. An extensor of the hand on the thumb side of the back of the forearm.

Lower iliac spine. A small prominence on the front border of the ilium, between the upper spine and the pubic bone.

Lŭm′bar. The region of the loins, or the portion between the ribs and the hipbone.

Mā′lar. The cheekbone.

Măllē′olus. The rounded projection on each bone of the leg at the ankle.

Măn′dible. The jawbone.

Masses, The three main. The skull, the rib cage, and the pelvis.

Măssē′ter. A large muscle on the side of the jaw, which raises the lower jaw and assists in mastication.

Măs′toid process. The prominence on the temporal bone behind the ear opening.

Maxilla (măk-sĭl′ ă). Bone of the upper jaw.

Mē′dian line. The surface line down the middle of the figure, corresponding to the axis.

Membranosus. Abbreviation for semimembranosus, which see.

Mĕtacär′pal. Beyond the carpals. Has reference to the five bones of the hand between the wristbones and the bones of the fingers.

Mĕtatär′sal. Beyond the tarsals. Refers to the five bones of the foot between the anklebones and the bones of the toes.

Nā′sal bones. Two small bones forming the bridge of the nose.

Oblique. The extensive muscular mass forming the lateral wall of the trunk.

Occĭp′ital. The bone forming the back plane of the skull.

Occĭp′itofrontā′lis. A thin sheet of muscle covering the skull from its base to the upper boundary of the eye sockets.

Olĕc′ranon. The process on the upper end of the ulna, forming the point of the elbow. Also the shallow depression in the lower end of the humerus into which the olecranon process fits when the elbow joint is extended.

Oppō′nens. One of the muscles of the little finger or the thumb, which draws the digit across the palm.

Orbĭc′ular. A circular muscle surrounding the eye or the mouth.

Ŏs căl′cis. The heelbone.

Ŏs măg′num. The large wristbone forming the middle of the arch of the wrist and connecting with the base of the metacarpal of the middle finger.

Outer văs′tus. One of the powerful quadriceps extensor muscles lying on the outer front part of the thigh.

Păl′mär. Pertaining to the palm of the hand.

Pălmā′ris. A superficial muscle of the forearm inserted in the palmar fascia.

Pàrĭ'etal. One of the broad curved bones on each side of the top surface of the skull.

Pàtĕl'la. The kneecap.

Pĕctorā'lis major. One of the two broad superficial muscles covering the chest.

Pĕctorā'lis minor. One of the two small chest muscles lying underneath the pectoralis majors.

Pĕl'vis. The basinlike hip girdle.

Pĕronē'us. One of the extensor muscles on the side of the leg.

Phalanx (fā' lănks), pl. *phalanges* (fā-lăn' jez). One of the digital bones of the hand or the foot.

Pĭ'siform. A small bone like a pea, on the ulnar and palm side of the wrist.

Platysma (plà-tĭz' mà). A broad, thin layer of muscle on each side of the neck and upper chest, which comes in evidence with the drawing down of the corners of the mouth.

Posterior spines. The prominences at the back of the iliac crests, usually marked by depressions.

Poupart's (pōō-pärz') *ligament*. The thickened lower boundary of the aponeurosis of the oblique muscle, forming the lower border of the abdomen.

Process. Any marked prominence or projecting part.

Pronā'tor. A muscle of the forearm, which rotates the hand to the palm-down position.

Pronā'tion. A rotation of the hand so that the palm is down (the arm being extended forward). The opposite of supination.

Pū'bic arch. The arch at the front, under part of the pelvis, formed by the pubic bones.

Pū'bis. The narrow, subcutaneous border of the pelvis, situated on the median line, at the base of the abdomen.

Quadrate (kwŏd' rāt). A group of several small muscles occupying the upper part of the front plane of the cheek.

Quadriceps (kwŏd' rĭ-sĕps) *extensor*. The group of four extensor muscles constituting the mass on the front of the thigh.

Rā'dial flexor. A forearm muscle attaching to the base of the index finger, *i.e.*, on the radius or thumb side.

Rā'dius. One of the two forearm bones. It is articulated with the ulna at both ends, so that it can partly revolve about that bone, carrying the hand with it.

Rĕc'tus abdŏm'inis. The long muscle of the abdomen extending from the pubis to the fifth, sixth, and seventh ribs.

Rĕc'tus fĕm'oris. The part of the quadriceps extensor running down the front of the thigh.

Rhŏm'boids. A deep mass of muscle connecting the cervical and upper dorsal vertebrae with the inner border of the scapula.

Rib cage. The shell formed by the ribs, dorsal vertebrae, and sternum.

Rough line of fē'mur. See Linea aspera.

Sā'croïl'iac triangle. The inverted triangle formed at the base of the spine by the posterior spines of the ilium and the lowest vertebra of the sacrum.

Sā'crum. The terminal segment of the vertebral column, which also forms part of the pelvis.

Sartō'rius. The long muscle crossing the thigh diagonally and used in drawing out the thigh, as in sitting like a tailor.

Scalēne'. A triangular group of small muscles running between the first two ribs and the second to sixth cervical vertebrae.

Scaphoid (skăf' oid). A carpal bone on the thumb side, articulating with the radius. Also a tarsal bone high on the inner side of the instep. Named from their shiplike form.

Scăp'ula. The shoulder blade.

Semilū'nar. One of the carpal, or wrist, bones, articulating with the radius and shaped like a half moon.

Semimembranō'sus. A large muscle, half membrane, on the back of the thigh, inner side. A flexor of the leg.

Semitendinō'sus. The half-tendinous muscle on the back of the thigh, inner side. A flexor of the leg.

Serrā'tus. The muscle on the side of the thorax and arising from the eight upper ribs by slips of saw-toothed character.

Seventh cĕr'vical vertebra. The prominent terminal vertebra of the cervical region, which limits the neck in back.

Short radial extensor. An extensor of the hand on the thumb side of the back of the forearm.

Shoulder girdle. The unit composed of the shoulder blades and collarbones, whose essential functions are to carry the armbones and to furnish attachment for muscles moving the arm.

Sĭg'moid cavity. The notch formed by the olecranon and coronoid processes of the ulna for articulation with the humerus.

Small trochăn'ter. The small prominence on the lower back part of the junction of the shaft with the neck of the femur.

Sō'leus. A broad, flat muscle on the calf, lying beneath the gastrocnemius.

Spinal column. The backbone, or spine.

Spine of scăp'ula. The sharp process running obliquely across the scapula to the cap of the shoulder and furnishing a landmark on the back.

Splē'nius. A muscle of the side and back of the neck, which belongs to the erector spinae mass.

Sternomastoid (stûr-nŏ-măs' toid). The prominent neck muscle running from the sternum and clavicle to the mastoid process.

Sternum (stûr' nŭm). The breastbone.

Stȳ'loid process. A prominence on the wrist end of the ulna or the radius. Also the slender process on the lower side of the temporal bone.

Subcutaneous. Those portions of the skeleton situated immediately beneath the skin and not covered by muscle.

Supercil′iary eminence. One of the two prominences on the frontal bone just above the inner portion of the eye socket.

Supinā′tion. A rotation of the hand so that the palm is turned up, or forward. The opposite of pronation.

Sū′pinator. A muscle that produces the movement of supination.

Suture. The line of union in immovable articulations, such as those between bones of the skull.

Tā′lus. The anklebone, which articulates with the tibia and the fibula to form the ankle joint.

Tär′sals. The seven bones that form the back half of the foot.

Tĕm′poral bone. The bone forming most of the side plane of the skull.

Tĕm′poral fŏs′sa. A shallow depression in the region of the temple above the zygomatic arch and in back of the eye orbit.

Tĕm′poral muscle. The fan-shaped muscle extending from the temporal ridge to the coronoid process of the mandible.

Tĕm′poral ridge. The ridge marking the change of plane between the top and side planes of the skull.

Tendinō′sus. Abbreviation for semitendinosus, which see.

Tĕn′don. A tough white cord of fibrous connective tissue uniting muscle with some other part and transmitting the force exerted by the muscle.

Tĕn′sor. A muscle that stretches a part or renders it tense. The tensor muscle flexes the thigh.

Tē′rēs mā′jor. A muscle connecting the scapula with the humerus and appearing as a rounded form on the scapula.

Tē′rēs mĭ′nor. A muscle of the shoulder located just above the teres major and partly covered by other muscles.

Thō′rax. The part of the trunk located between the neck and the base of the rib cage.

Thumb, Extensors of. The muscles on the thumb side of the wrist whose tendons are conspicuous when the thumb is extended.

Thyroid. Shield shape. The name of the neck cartilage, prominent in the male and known as the *Adam's apple;* also the name of the neck gland more conspicuous in the female.

Tĭb′ia. The shinbone.

Tibiā′lis. The muscle passing down the outer front of the tibia, which flexes the ankle.

Trapē′zium. A carpal bone at the base of the thumb. Its face is of irregular four-sided type.

Trapē′zius. The broad superficial muscle covering the upper back.

Trăp′ezoid. A carpal bone at the base of the index finger. Like the geometrical figure, its face has two sides parallel.

Trī'ceps. The three-headed extensor muscle forming the mass of the back of the arm.

Trochăn'ter. See Great trochanter and Small trochanter.

Trochlea (trŏk' lē-à). The pulleylike surface on the humerus that furnishes articulation with the ulna.

Tŭ'bercle. A small, bony prominence for the attachment of muscle or ligament.

Tuberŏs'ity. A large prominence serving for the attachment of muscles or ligaments.

Ŭl'na. The bone of the forearm which, with the humerus, forms the elbow joint.

Ŭl'nar extensor. A muscle located on the ulnar or little-finger side of the forearm and acting to straighten the wrist.

Ŭl'nar flexor. A muscle located on the little-finger side of the forearm and acting to bend the wrist.

Ŭn'ciform. A hook-shaped carpal bone at the bases of the third and little fingers.

Upper ĭl'ĭăc spine. The subcutaneous prominence on the front upper end of the iliac crest.

Văs'tus. The name of two large muscles of the thigh, which extend the leg.

Vertebra, pl. *vertebrae* (vûr' tĕ-brē). One of the 24 bony segments composing the spinal column.

Y ligament. See Iliofemoral.

Zygomatic (zī-gŏ-măt' ĭk). A cheek muscle attached to the corner of the mouth and acting to produce the smile.

Zygomatic arch. The arch of bone running from the cheekbone to the region of the ear opening.

INDEX

A

Abduction, defined, 134n.
Action, 177
  first principle of, 16, 19, 178
  of head, 29
  other conditions of, 178–180
Adduction, defined, 134n.
Adductor of thumb, 169, Pl. 45
Adductors of thigh, 140, Pl. 36
Anconeus, 160, Pl. 42
Ankle bones, 61, Pl. 16
Annular ligament, 150, 168
Arm, muscles of, 156, Pls. 41, 42
  and thigh muscles compared, 161–162
  muscles moving, 112, Pls. 29, 30
Armpit, muscular relations of, 160, Pl. 42
Atlas, 33, Pl. 4

B

Biceps, of arm, 156, Pl. 41
Biceps femoris, 139, Pl. 35
Bones, of ankle, 61, Pl. 16
  classification of, 21

Bones, of face, 23, Pl. 3
  of foot, 61, Pl. 16
    compared with bones of hand, 63
  of forearm, 69, Pl. 18
  of hand, 75, Pls. 20, 21
    compared with bones of foot, 63
  of leg, 57, Pl. 14
  of skull, 23, Pl. 3
  of wrist and palm, 75, Pl. 20
Bony structure, 20
Brachialis, 159, Pl. 41
Buccinator, 93, Pl. 24

C

Carpals, 75, Pl. 20
Charcoal technique, 103
Classification, of bones, 21
  of muscles, 88
    of trunk, 124
Clavicle, 40, 43, Pls. 7–9
Coccyx, 34, Pls. 4, 10–12
Compressor, 94, Pl. 24
Condyle, defined, 22
Construction, of ear, 100
  of eye, 97
  of figure in action, 180

Construction, of figure in action, in
    simple movement, 19
  of foot, 65, 153
  of hand, 81, 170
  of head, 28
  of hip and thigh, 147
  of lower limb, 64
  of male figure, front, 14
    profile, 36
  of mouth, 101
  nature of, 7
  of neck, 129
  of nose, 99
  of skull, 25–26
  of trunk, 51
  of upper limb, 83, 175
Contour, significance of, 94
Contractive muscles of face, 94, Pl. 24
Coraco, 159, Pl. 41
Corrugator, 94, Pl. 24
Cuboid, 63, Pl. 16
Cuneiforms of foot, 63, Pl. 16

D

Deep flexors of fingers and thumb,
    164, Pl. 44
Deltoid, 118, Pl. 30
Depressor, 94, Pl. 24
Dorsal interossei, 170, Pl. 45
Drapery, 181

E

Ear, construction of, 100
Edges, handling of, 105

Elbow joint, 71, Pl. 19
Erector spinae, 107, Pl. 25
Expansive muscles of face, 93, Pl. 24
Extensors, of fingers, 167, Pl. 44
  of leg, 138, Pl. 35
  of thumb, 164, Pl. 43
  of toes, 149, Pl. 39
  of wrist and of fingers, 167, Pl. 44
Eye, construction of, 97

F

Face, muscles of, 90, Pl. 24
  planes of, 27, 30
  proportions of, 26
Features, 97
Female figure, characteristics of, 14,
    Pl. 2
  compared with male, 9, Pls. 1, 2
  proportions of, 14, Pl. 2
Femur, 54, Pl. 13
Fibula, 58, Pl. 14
Fingers, compared with toes, 82
Flexors, and adductors of thumb and
    of little finger, 169, Pl. 45
  of leg, 139, Pl. 35
  of toes, 150, Pl. 39
  of wrist 164, Pl. 44
Foot, bones of, 61, Pl. 16
  construction of, 65, 153
  phalanges of, 61, Pl. 16
  structure of, 153
Forearm, bones of, 69, Pl. 18
  muscles of, 163, Pls. 43, 44
Fossa, defined, 22

Frontal bone, 23, Pl. 3

G

Gastrocnemius, 149, Pl. 38
Gluteus maximus, 132, Pl. 33
Gluteus medius, 134, Pl. 33
Gracilis, 140, Pl. 36

H

Hair, structure and construction of, 95
Hand, bones of, 75, Pls. 20, 21
    construction of, 81, 170
    muscles of, 169, Pl. 45
Head, construction of, 28–29
    muscles of, 90, Pls. 23, 24
    and neck, relations of, 31
    perspective of, 31
    planes of, 27, 30
    prominences and depressions of, 27
Hip, compared with shoulder, 137
    muscles of, 132, Pls. 33, 34
    and thigh, construction of, 147
        muscles of, correlated, 144, Pl. 37
Hip girdle, 46, Pls. 10–12
Human figure, nature of, 5
Humerus, 67, Pl. 17
Hyoid bone, 126
Hyoid muscles, 126

I

Iliofemoral, or Y ligament, 51
Iliopsoas, 137, Pl. 34
Iliotibial band, 132
Ilium, 46, Pl. 10

Infant, proportions of, 34
Infraspinatus and teres minor, 118, Pl. 29
Inner vastus, 138, Pl. 35
Intermuscular septum, 160
Interossei, dorsal, 170, Pl. 45
    palmar, 170, Pl. 45
Ischial tuberosity, 49
Ischium, 46, 49, Pls. 11, 12

J

Joints, effect of bones at, 20–21

K

Knee joint, 60, Pl. 15

L

Latissimus dorsi, 121, Pl. 29
Leg, bones of, 57, Pl. 14
    extensors of, 138, Pl. 35
    flexors of, 139, Pl. 35
    muscles of, 148, Pls. 38–40
        correlation of, 153
Levator, 112, Pl. 27
Long peroneus, 148, Pl. 38
Long radial extensor, 167, Pl. 44
Lower limb, bones and masses of, 54
    construction of, 64

M

Malar bones, 23, Pl. 3
Male figure, compared with female, 9, Pls. 1, 2
    process of construction of, 14

Male figure, proportions of, 11, Pl. 1

Mandible, 25, Pl. 3

Masseter, 90, Pl. 23

Materials and technique, pencil, 8

Maxilla, 25, Pl. 3

Membranosus (*see* Semimembranosus)

Metacarpals, 76, Pl. 20

Metatarsals, 61, Pl. 16

Modeling, principle of, 104

Mouth, construction of, 101

Movement in the figure, 16, 178

Movements, of shoulder girdle, 44

    of spinal column, 35

    of supination and pronation, 79, Pl. 22

Muscles, of arm, 156, Pls. 41, 42

    classification of, 88

    of face, 90, Pl. 24

        contractive, 94, Pl. 24

        expansive, 93, Pl. 24

    of forearm, 163, Pls. 43, 44

    of hand, 169, Pl. 45

    of head, 90, Pls. 23, 24

    of hip, 132, Pls. 33, 34

    of leg, 148, Pls. 38–40

        correlation of, 153, Pl. 40

    of lower limb, summary of, 155

    moving arm, 112

    moving leg, 138, Pl. 35

    moving trunk, 107, Pls. 25, 26

    nature of, 87

    of neck, 125, Pl. 31

    of thigh, 138, Pls. 35–37

    of trunk, complete, 130, Pl. 32

Muscles, of upper limb, correlated, 174, Pl. 46

    summary of, 174

Muscular relations of armpit, 160, Pl. 42

N

Nasal bones, 25, Pl. 16

Neck, construction of, 129

    muscles of, 125, Pl. 31

Nose, construction of, 99

O

Oblique, 111, Pl. 26

Occipital, 23, Pl. 3

Occipitofrontalis, 94, Pl. 24

Opponens, of little finger, 169, Pl. 45

    of thumb, 169, Pl. 45

Orbicular, of eye, 94, Pl. 24

    of mouth, 94, Pl. 24

Os calcis, 61, Pl. 16

Outer vastus, 138, Pl. 35

P

Palmar interossei, 170, Pl. 45

Palmaris, 164, Pl. 44

Parietal, 23, Pl. 3

Patella, 58, Pl. 15

Pectoralis major, 122, Pl. 30

Pectoralis minor, 112, Pl. 27

Pelvis, 46, Pls. 10–12

Perspective of head, 31

Phalanges, of foot, 61, Pl. 16

    of hand, 79, Pl. 21

Planes, of face, 27
Platysma, 126
Portraiture, 105
Poupart's ligament, 111, Pl. 34
Process, defined, 22
Prominences and depressions of head, 27
Pronation, 79, Pl. 22
Pronator, 163, Pl. 43
Proportion, nature of, 9
Proportions, of face, 26
    of female figure, 14, Pl. 2
    of male figure, 11, Pl. 1
Pubis, 46, 49, Pls. 10, 11

Q

Quadrate, 93, Pl. 24
Quadriceps extensor, 138, Pl. 35

R

Radial flexor, 164, Pl. 44
Radius, 69, 71, Pl. 18
Rectus abdominis, 108, Pl. 26
Rectus femoris, 138, Pl. 35
Rhomboids, 112, Pl. 27
Rib cage, 36, Pls. 5, 6
Ribs, 38, Pls. 5, 6

S

Sacrum, 34, Pls. 4, 10–12
Sartorius, 140, Pl. 36
Scalene, 125, Pl. 31
Scaphoid, 63, Pl. 16
Scapula, 40, Pls. 7–9
Semimembranosus, 139, Pl. 35

Semitendinosus, 139, Pl. 35
Serratus, 113, Pl. 27
Seventh cervical, 33, Pl. 4
Short extensor of toes, 150, Pl. 40
Short peroneus, 148, Pl. 38
Short radial extensor, 167, Pl. 44
Shoulder, compared with hips, 137
Shoulder girdle, 40, Pl. 7
    movements of, 44
Skull, bones of, 23, Pl. 3
    construction of, 25–26
Soleus, 149, Pl. 38
Spinal column, 33, Pl. 4
    movements of, 35
Splenius, 129, Pl. 32
Sternomastoid, 125, Pl. 31
Sternum, 40, Pls. 5, 6
Structure and construction, of foot, 153
    of hair, 95
Subcutaneous, defined, 20
Supination and pronation, 79, Pl. 22
Supinator, 163, Pl. 43
Sutures, 25

T

Talus, 61, Pl. 16
Tarsals, 61, Pl. 16
Technique, charcoal, 103
    of handling edges, 105
    pencil, 8
Temporal bone, 23, Pl. 3
Temporal muscle, 90, Pl. 23
Tendinosus (see Semitendinosus)
Tensor, 133, Pl. 33
Teres major, 118, Pl. 29

Teres minor, 118, Pl. 29

Thigh, compared with arm, 161–162
  muscles of, 138, Pls. 35–37

Thighbone, 54, Pl. 13

Thumb, power of opposition in, 76

Thyroid cartilage, 126

Thyroid gland, 126

Tibia, 57, Pl. 14

Tibialis, 148, Pl. 38

Toes, compared with fingers, 82

Trapezius, 114, Pl. 28

Triceps, 159, Pl. 42

Trunk, bones and masses of, 33, Pls.
  4–9
  construction of, 51
  muscles moving, 107, Pls. 25, 26
  muscular structure of, 130, Pl. 32

Tubercle, defined, 22

Tuberosity, defined, 22

U

Ulna, 69, Pl. 18

Ulnar extensor, 167, Pl. 44

Ulnar flexor, 164, Pl. 44

Upper limb, bones and masses of, 67,
  Pls. 17, 18
  construction of, 83, 175
  muscles of, 156

V

Vasti, inner and outer, 138, Pl. 35

Vertebrae, 33, Pl. 4

W

White line, 108, Pl. 26

Wrist, bones of, 75, Pl. 20
  movements of, 79

Y

Y ligament, 51

Z

Zygomatic arch, 25, Pl. 3

Zygomatic muscle, 93, Pl. 24